AIRFIX
magazine guide 11

RAF Camouflage
of
World War 2

Michael J F Bowyer

Patrick Stephens Ltd
in association with Airfix Products Ltd

First published – November 1975

ISBN 0 85059 215 1

Don't forget these other Airfix Magazine Guides!

No 1 *Plastic Modelling*
by Gerald Scarborough
No 2 *Aircraft Modelling*
by Bryan Philpott
No 3 *Military Modelling*
by Gerald Scarborough
No 4 *Napoleonic Wargaming*
by Bruce Quarrie
No 5 *Tank & AFV Modelling*
by Gerald Scarborough
No 6 *RAF Fighters of World War 2*
by Alan W. Hall
No 7 *Warship Modelling*
by Peter Hodges
No 8 *German Tanks of World War 2*
by Terry Gander and
Peter Chamberlain
No 9 *Ancient Wargaming*
by Phil Barker
No 10 *Luftwaffe Camouflage
of World War 2*
by Bryan Philpott
No 12 *Afrika Korps*
by Bruce Quarrie

Cover design by Tim McPhee

Text set in 8 on 9 pt Helvetica Medium by Blackfriars Press Limited, Leicester.
Printed on Fineblade cartridge 90 gm² and bound by The Garden City Press Limited, Letchworth, Herts.
Published by Patrick Stephens Limited, Bar Hill, Cambridge CB3 8EL, in association with Airfix Products Limited, London SW18.

Contents

Acknowledgement

In compiling this book I have had the help of Michael Sayers, a young modeller able to tell me the sort of thing he, and doubtless many like him, would want to know. To him I am also grateful for letting me know which parts of the original draft he found difficult to understand.

Editor's introduction

This volume attempts to outline, especially for young people, the basic marking schemes used on RAF aircraft during World War 2. Drawing on his own notes made at the time, as well as official and other sources, Michael Bowyer has, at the same time, written an authoritative ready-reference for the serious aviation enthusiast and modeller at a price which all can afford.

Aircraft markings are a source of continuous fascination and, although fighters and bombers are always the most popular subjects, the author has also included details of the markings applied to other types, such as trainers, transport, reconnaissance, coastal and target-towing machines, to name a few — information which is not easily found elsewhere. Readers wishing to delve more deeply into the subjects of fighter or bomber markings are recommended to the two other books by the same author, and published by Patrick Stephens: *Fighting Colours 1937-1975* and *Bombing Colours 1937-73*.

One final word of caution should be made here. Although, throughout aviation history, there have been laid down rules and regulations for the painting of aircraft, there are always exceptions. Problems of paint supply, of repairing battle-damaged machines, and with the simple artistic capabilities of the man applying the paint, all lead to differences even between aircraft of the same type, production batch and squadron. As a result the modeller needs to be very careful when painting his kits, and should seek out as many photographs and references for the particular machine he is attempting to portray before plunging his brush into the paint tin.

BRUCE QUARRIE

Camouflage introduced

one which they belonged within their squadron.

Training aircraft were also silver, but in July 1936 these were ordered to be painted yellow overall apart from the metal engine cowling panels. These latter were left in natural finish and usually polished. Later, those aircraft set aside to tow targets for gunnery practice had broad black diagonal stripes applied overall on the yellow base.

These were the colours of peace.

Camouflage and markings on military aircraft serve two main purposes. They hide aircraft when seen from above or below, and are a useful identifying feature for friendly forces.

Camouflage in war is quite new. Bright uniforms used to be important for the identity of regiments and nationalities in battle. With the development of aerial observation armies have learnt to hide themselves, and camouflage now plays a vital part against elaborate aerial reconnaissance.

In World War 1 camouflage came into its own on aeroplanes of the Royal Flying Corps, whose khaki-browns and clear doped creamy undersides brought useful proof of its value. During the 1920s and 1930s many RAF aircraft were all silver. Without an enemy it made sense for the aircraft to be easily seen. Silver was nevertheless a sensible colour, giving some disguise when seen against clouds. Fighter squadrons, keeping the ideas of Army regiments, adopted colourful squadron markings in 1926, and these were painted on the fuselage sides and upper wing surfaces so that pilots could easily identify their squadron mates.

Heavy bombers of the RAF were camouflaged in a dark green shade called Nivo to make them as invisible as possible at night. They had only blue and red night flying roundels, for a white ring would have revealed them.

Aircraft operating over the sea were silver. Some had squadron numbers in black or in the colour of the Flight to

When large expansion of the RAF took place in the mid-1930s, matt camouflage was ordered for all operational aircraft. The Air Ministry issued camouflage patterns varying according to aircraft size. Two colour shades were chosen representing dark and light land areas, the dark represented by Dark Green and the other by Dark Earth, a brown shade. These colours, commonly referred to at the time as 'sand and spinach', formed the Temperate Land Scheme, ie the colours for use in temperate latitudes, although a number of aircraft sent to tropical regions retained them. A Temperate Sea Scheme was also devised using Dark Slate Grey (a greenish shade) and Extra Dark Sea Grey, which was introduced in 1939 replacing temporary use of the Land Scheme.

Under surfaces of fighters would remain silver, those of bombers would be black. Fighters had blue-white-red underwing roundels and black aircraft serial numbers. Bombers wore no underwing roundels but had white serials on their under surfaces. In April 1937 an official order stated that all operational aircraft would leave factories in camouflage colours, although aircraft built late in 1936 already had this finish.

To make the aircraft easy to see in peacetime, fuselage and upper wing roundels in glossy paint were outlined yellow. On bombers, the squadron number and a letter to identify the aircraft were ordered to be a medium shade of grey, although some squadrons for a time carried theirs in yellow. Fighters similarly marked sometimes had their squadron number in Flight colour of red, blue or yellow and sometimes green.

Ansons of Coastal Command for a while retained an all-silver finish like flying-boats. A few Ansons had their serials in black above their wings. Unit markings were black or in Flight colour. Ansons leaving the Manchester factory in summer 1937 were completed in bomber camouflage which they still had when used by Coastal Command.

The next major changes came in September 1938 when war nearly broke out during the Munich crisis. Biplane fighters still in use were hurriedly camouflaged. An assortment of camouflage markings were quickly applied to operational aircraft. Some then had matt blue and red roundels (known as Type B) painted on their sides and upper surfaces, and some had serial numbers and squadron markings painted over, for security reasons. Units applied grey identity (or 'code' letters) to some aircraft, two letters indicating the squadron with a single letter to identify each individual aircraft. These letters, to no code system as such, were needed to allow aircraft to keep formation during operations, or to offer a radio call sign.

Much confusion followed the Emergency. Some squadrons kept their codes and blue/red roundels, whilst others went back to the old styles. Others had made no changes and such inconsistency in markings has remained.

A modeller wishing to add to his collection aircraft of the immediate pre-war period is likely to find suitable finishes difficult to discover in detail, unless he relies upon well-known photographs. Strict bans on photography then existed, and few photographs were taken even officially. Such photography as took place was usually undertaken using orthochromatic film not very sensitive to yellows and reds. Prints from such negatives make the reds and yellows look black, and this may be misleading to a modeller new to his hobby.

A visit to a pre-war RAF station of the late thirties showed an interesting feature of camouflage. On each type of aircraft there were two possible patterns of camouflage, one the mirror image of the other and applied to alternately built machines. Usually aircraft with even numbered serials had the 'A' pattern, the others 'B' Pattern. This style of finish continued at the factories until January 1941, although exceptions to the ruling took place as, for example, on Fairey Battle bombers. Heyford, Virginia and Hendon bombers kept their Nivo finish until they left the squadrons, and biplane fighters wore individualistic camouflage patterns.

Close examination of the aircraft showed the camouflage paint to be very rough when touched, thick and very matt so that the aeroplanes gave the impression of being very badly finished, this always seeming to be more true of bombers than fighters.

Official painting orders stated that code letters would be four feet high in six-inch strokes, but again there were many anomalies as units made their letters as bold as they considered possible. Letter shapes varied too, as they did throughout the war.

Some squadrons displayed their identity by applying a squadron badge painted on the fin on a spearhead shape in the case of fighters like the Hurricanes of No 56 Squadron, and on a grenade shape in the case of bombers like the Blenheims of No 114 Squadron. Army co-operation aircraft had theirs on a six pointed star, like the Hectors of No 59 Squadron. These markings were gradually removed because they broke the secrecy given by the then-secret code letters.

All-yellow trainers showed up very brightly on the ground. Late in 1938 Flying Training Schools began to paint the upper surfaces of their aircraft Dark Green and Dark Earth, the camouflage extending only a short way down the fuselage sides. Individual identity was usually by means of a black number amidships, or on the aircraft's nose, which was now camouflaged with yellow sides. Even among trainers there were the usual exceptions for Battles and Ansons in use at Elementary and Reserve Flying Training Schools kept bomber colours whilst having grey or yellow individual identity numbers or letters.

The first production Short Sunderland flying-boats were delivered all-silver. Before camouflage came into use instructions had been issued that flying-boats would have silver painted wings and grey hulls. Supermarine Scapas had this scheme, but it seems unlikely that it was ever applied to Short Singapores and Saro Londons although some Stranraers had it. By spring 1939 Sunderlands were leaving the production line in Temperate Land Scheme with blue/red roundels and black under surfaces which carried white serials.

Into the war army co-operation squadrons flew Hector biplanes. Their replacement type was the Westland Lysander, the first production examples of which wore Dark Green/Dark Earth camouflage and silver under surfaces which bore blue/white/red roundels and black serials.

Autumn 1938 did not only see a change in roundels and unit identity markings. It was then that a few fighters appeared with white and black under surfaces, a useful camouflage feature as the aircraft flitted between grey and bright skies. At the same time it was a help to the defences for recognition purposes. It came into widespread use early in 1939. Orders were that the port half of the under surfaces should be black and the rest white. Sometimes these colours were reversed, and often they met at other than the central line of the fuselage under surfaces. In some cases factory finished fighters had the entire under surfaces of their noses, and sometimes rear fuselages too, painted silver. No underwing roundels or serial numbers should have been carried, but there were exceptions to this. Some aircraft had their ailerons painted in the reverse colour to the wings. Since the aircraft used for army co-operation were then under the control of Fighter Command these aircraft were also given black/white under surfaces.

Models of aircraft of the period just before the war are uncommon, so they are always interesting items in any collection. When painting the very matt camouflage and glossy yellow/blue/white/red roundels a rule to observe is that the meeting line of the colours is clear. The merged colours often specified have always been a rare feature on RAF aircraft.

Black eight-inch serial numbers were usually carried on the rudders of all aircraft to the start of the war, the preceding letter being above the digits. Although many were then removed, at the time when white underwing serials were painted out on bombers, some aircraft kept rudder serials well into 1940. There were also traces of the yellow outer rings to roundels being painted over when blue and red areas were extended to meet over the previous white portions. Some factory finished fighters had very small roundels on wings and fuselages, and some Hurricanes and Spitfires had only one wing roundel. The pitfalls to watch for on models of the expansion period are many.

two

Home-based fighters

Wartime fighter camouflage fell, broadly, into six main groupings. When war began, home-based fighter aircraft wore Dark Green and Dark Earth camouflage with black and white under surfaces, as in pre-war days. Squadron letters were in an assortment of mid-greys and propeller spinners were black. About half the aircraft still had rudder serials, a feature seen well into 1940.

At the end of May 1940 new under surface colours began to appear. Day bombers had been repainted in a pale greenish blue shade known as Camo-tint, later Duck Egg Blue, Duck Egg Green or Sky — you can take your pick. There had been much experimentation with this before the war began and eventually a shade made from white with a small amount of yellow and a dash of Prussian Blue was adopted. The name Duck Egg Green has always seemed to me the most logical to describe the colour on account of its greenish tone.

Being a completely new colour for paint stores at the fighter stations to stock it was soon in very short supply. Many stations had to mix their own paint as a result of which there were soon many shades of the new tone ranging from quite rich blues almost like Azure Blue to colours best described as light green, as each station tried to produce paint in the tone listed by the SBOAC formula. The change was ordered to take place fully from June 7 1940, but in reality it took many weeks to repaint the fighters. Even during the middle of the Battle of Britain some still had black/white

Defiant N1673 on a maker's test flight and wearing Dark Green/Dark Earth camouflage with Sky under surfaces flew briefly on operations from Rochford with 264 Squadron August 25 to September 4 1940. It was presumably re-sprayed black overall before service with 141 Squadron April 11 to May 16 1941. It was with 2 Air Gunnery School August 14 1941 to June 6 1942 when it joined No 277 ASR Squadron who returned it to 2 AGS on December 31 1942 with whom it stayed until August 3 1943. It was written off September 14 1943.

Long absent from publication has been a shot of a Mosquito II of No 157 Squadron, seen here evidenced by RS:B-W4087 with Dull Red codes and serials on its Special Night finish. Note the narrow outline to the fuselage roundel. The aircraft was later fitted with a Turbinlite (Kyle Webster).

Hurricane N2359 served with 17 Squadron from June 6 to August 25 1940. Note Sky under surfaces and Sky spinner. It joined No 6 (Fighter) OTU August 25 1940 and was burnt out in a flying accident on June 11 1941 (L. W. Stevens).

Shots of Battle of Britain Spitfires are rare. This, from P. Scott, shows a machine of 609 Squadron said to have been photographed at Northolt. Note the large fuselage serial, Medium Grey codes and the very small wing roundel. The serial, barely visible on the original print, looks like 'X44 . .'

Awaiting a call for action are three Mosquito FB VIs of No 487 Squadron, all in Dark Green/Medium Sea Grey finish. Although a basic outline of marking schemes is possible, aircraft often varied in detail, HX972:EG-P nearest, for instance, having one Sky spinner. It served with the squadron from November 1943 until written off after a flying accident on May 28 1944 (via R. Kitching).

under surfaces. Before May was out some stations had painted the under surfaces of their Spitfires silver, presumably as an interim measure.

Stage three in the markings pattern came during the winter of 1940/41 with the decision to paint aircraft used for night fighting in an overall very rough matt black called Special Night. No fighters had been purely employed at night until September 1940. Experience showed their need for a dark camouflage. Squadron letters and serials varied from white through very pale greys to Sky.

During December 1940 the all-black night fighters began to appear in some numbers. They usually looked very scruffy, partly because oil affected the paint. It is known that some night fighters were temporarily painted overall in a black distemper wash applied over existing camouflage and roundels. In the autumn of 1941 code letters changed to Dull Red, a colour with a brownish appearance, which was also used for serial numbers. As early as April 1941 Dull Red serials were in use. The black finish remained on night fighters until the autumn of 1942.

December 1940 also saw the addition of an 18-inch wide Sky band around the fuselage immediately ahead of the tailplane on day fighters,

whose spinners were also ordered to be Sky. By now supplies of Sky were being received from the paint manufacturers and these often contrasted with the shades used for the under surfaces of fighters.

December 1940 saw stage four, a return to half black undersides, port under surfaces being temporarily black. This was ordered to be removed on February 18, ground defences being advised of the change. Some fighters were then seen to be flying without black under surfaces, but there seems to have been some halt to the change and it appears that not until April was it finally ordered to be removed. There was thus a confused situation with some fighters half black and others Sky. Squadron letters remained medium grey.

Stage five in wartime fighter markings came in the summer of 1941. Fighter squadrons had, since January, been increasingly active over France during bomber escort missions, large formation sweeps and in pairs flying 'rhubarbs' during which they shot up targets of opportunity. For the most part, though, fighter squadrons found themselves persistently covering inshore convoys and ships entering and leaving British ports, and patrolling over major anchorages like Scapa Flow. Thus, Fighter Command found

Spitfire XIV RB144 has standard fighter finish with a yellow leading edge band on its slightly glossy camouflage. Photographèd at Hatfield on November 21 1944, RB144 was used for propeller tests and here is fitted with a contra-prop.

itself very much marine-orientated and camouflage was accordingly changed.

In May 1941 Hurricanes of No 56 Squadron were ordered to test an assortment of grey shades on areas once Dark Earth. Part of the trials included painting the Hurricanes two shades of grey on their upper surfaces, whilst a lighter grey was chosen for the under surfaces. Code letters remained Medium Sea Grey.

Trials continued during June 1941 until it was eventually decided to paint fighter aircraft Medium Sea Grey on their under surfaces while the upper surfaces were Dark Green and a dark shade of grey. The tone finally selected for the latter was bluish, called Ocean Grey, but stocks of this were for some months in short supply. Instead, stations went ahead producing their own dark grey in a variety of shades just as they had done when mixing Sky. At others Dark Sea Grey was applied, as at Duxford, Debden and Coltishall. Sky spinners and rear fuselage bands were retained, and squadron codes were now Sky too.

Instructions were issued that the colours would become standard for day fighters from August 21, and the change to grey-green finish took place rapidly. Apart from detail changes, this scheme remained to the end of the war. In its later stages the paints used had a much smoother, slightly shiny finish. If polished they took on a dis-

tinctly glossy appearance although were never as glossy as the post-war paints. By 1944 the shade of Sky in common use was very pale, indeed often it looked almost white.

A useful identity feature for RAF fighters when seen head on was a narrow yellow stripe along the outer edges of both mainplanes, this being introduced at the start of July 1942.

The final major alteration to camouflage came in the case of night fighters. After trials and operational flying using the all-black machines, that colour was seen to be not so ideal as was first thought. Even at the time of its introduction a dark shade of green had met preference. In moonlight, and during operations in high latitudes, black gave a silhouette effect, and the very rough finish of Special Night cut performance — especially of the Mosquito. Accordingly a variety of combinations of grey-green-bluish grey and even brown were tried. Finally it was agreed that a scheme of disruptive Medium Sea Grey and Dark Green would be applied to upper surfaces and Medium Sea Grey to the lower surfaces from October 1942. Serial numbers would be black (sometimes Dull Red), squadron codes Dull Red. Since night fighters were sometimes to be employed by day — notably over the Bay of Biscay and on intruder type sorties — the new scheme seemed the best compromise.

Home-based fighters

From May 1943 day fighters with high-altitude performance were finished on production lines with Medium Sea Grey upper surfaces and tail surfaces and PR Blue under surfaces. Roundels on these machines were Type B and the fin stripes were blue and red. Such markings applied to Spitfire VIIs, some Mk IXs, Hornets, some Vampires and some Welkins although a few of the latter wore night fighter camouflage.

An interesting saga surrounded the colour of codes on Air-Sea Rescue aircraft. Originally their codes were Sky, then they changed to Dull Red. To make the Spitfires readily identifiable to crews flying aircraft on offensive operations, the codes on the ASR Spitfires were changed to yellow in February 1943. As a special marking these aircraft carried a tapering black line under their fuselages from the spinner to the rudder post. Ansons, Oxfords, Lysanders and Warwicks used for ASR duty are all known to have had yellow codes, but on Walruses and Sea Otters they were generally Dull Red to the end of the war.

One other series of 'code' letters deserves mention. Fighter wing leaders were allowed to paint their initials on their aircraft so that combinations appeared that lay outside the system, and this could be confusing to any modeller.

On January 3 1945, after the sudden air attack on the European bases of the 2nd Tactical Air Force, Sky tail bands were painted out and spinners

Top *Meteor FIII EE243 was with No 616 Squadron from January 19 1945 until it passed to the Air Fighting Development Unit at Wittering, still coded YQ:U. Note the red 'U' on the nose-wheel door and standard fighter camouflage without yellow leading edge bands.* **Above** *A Gladiator KW:S of No 615 Squadron in France early in 1940. Dark Green/Dark Earth/black/ white finish with Medium Grey codes and Type A fuselage roundel. Rudder stripes were not worn by the Gladiator (K. Belcher).*

were usually painted Ocean Grey or black. A white ring was introduced in the upper wing roundels as an aid to identity now that the Sky trim had been removed.

Shortly before hostilities ceased in Europe some Mustang IVs joined the RAF in natural (ie silver metal) finish, and even before this a few Spitfires were flying in bare metal finish. Silver, natural or aluminium finish really belonged to the post-war era.

three

Home-based bombers

When war commenced all bombers, apart from some employed for training purposes, wore matt Dark Green/Dark Earth/Night (ie black) finish. This was strange really for it was envisaged that the bombers would operate mainly by day except for the Whitleys. Their colours, however, suited them to night operations, black being an anti-searchlight feature.

In July 1939 Bomber Command pointed out that black was an unsuit-

An interesting photograph of a Mosquito B20 KB161 named VANCOUVER British Columbia Canada (in white). The Sky spinners and fuselage band are unusual. KB161 arrived in Britain in September 1943 and served with No 139 Squadron from November 1943, making the Mk 20's first operational flight on December 2 1943. Coded XD:H, KB161 crashed on return from operations May 10/11 1944 and was burnt out.

able colour for day bomber under surfaces. It suggested that silver, light blue-grey or a combination of such colours would be better. Colours similar to those on fighters were suggested for reconnaissance aircraft. Experiments were meanwhile under way to produce a super-matt black finish for bomber under surfaces, extended up the fuselage sides and over the fins and rudders. The effectiveness of the new paint, removable with petrol thus allowing a lighter day finish perhaps to replace it, was proven in trials. At the outbreak of war Bomber Command requested supplies of this new dope. These were limited and initial quantities available were sent to the four Whitley stations. From these bases night operations would be conducted.

Further trials were conducted in October 1939 using a Whitley 5 of 77 Squadron which was difficult to see even in a searchlight beam. Painting of the Whitley force with the new dope then went ahead, albeit slowly for even in mid-1940 Whitleys in squadron hands still awaited the ultra-matt finish. Squadron codes remained medium grey whilst fuselage serials (and fin serials, where retained) were black.

While the new night finish was tested work continued on devising a new under surface shade for day bombers. Titanine produced Camotint making the aircraft difficult to spot against the sky. A number of blue

shades were devised until eventually a pale green shade was adopted after flight trials, mainly from Heston. No 2 Group operating Blenheims was looking into means of streamlining them by filling cracks, etc. It complained about the rough finish of dope, and when the new pale green shade was made available this had a much smoother texture. The combination of this and streamlining generally improved the performance of the Blenheims, but it was costly in man hours to produce. Nos 114 and 139 Squadrons at Wyton were first to have the treatment. Further considerations led to the application of the new paint shade and streamlining to only a limited number of so-called 'polished' Blenheims used for operations where speed was essential. Medium grey code letters were retained on these aircraft.

The Fairey Battles of the Advanced Air Striking Force in France retained Dark Green/Dark Earth/black finish for the intention was to replace them with Blenheims, although in the event only Nos 114 and 139 Squadrons were involved and the black Battles continued in use until June 1940.

During summer 1940 the ultra-matt black finish was extended to Hampden and Wellington bombers, but it took some months to complete. The ease with which the dope could be removed by oil and petrol splash, and very rapid weathering, produced some extremely shabby looking aircraft. The earlier matt black often showed through, and patching with either types of paint added to the desultory appearance.

What made the bombers even more drab was a gradual extension, from mid-1940, of black. Firstly it was taken half way up the fuselage sides ending in broad sweeps. It extended finally to about three-quarters of the way up the fuselage and eventually over the fins and rudders. All this was done in an attempt to defeat the effectiveness of searchlights, through belts of which most night sorties against Germany had to pass. In December 1940 black sides and tails were ordered for all bombers although the new types just entering service did not acquire them until some weeks of 1941 had passed.

International identity markings were toned down by the overpainting of the white fuselage rings and white in the fin stripes, but squadron codes remained light or medium grey. On the black areas serials became grey,

Wellington 1c SR:P:R3295 forced landed on Schiermonikoog during an operation against Hamburg on November 30/December 1 1941. The black wavy line so common on bombers is in evidence and the Medium Grey codes (via G. J. Zwanenburg).

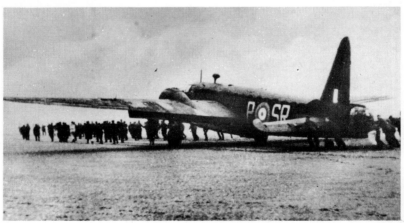

RAF Camouflage of World War 2

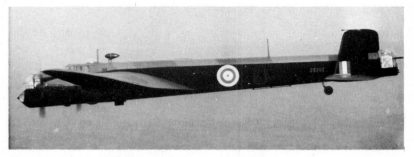

A standard production Whitley V with red serial Z9302. It had an eventful career with Nos 77, 78, 51 Squadrons and No 10 OTU. This machine has the straight line ending to the black area which became general in 1942.

although some aircraft had Dull Red serials in the winter of 1940/41.

The new breed of bombers — the Stirling, Manchester and Halifax — entered service in ultra-matt black (Special Night) with Temperate Land Scheme upper surfaces. Early in 1941 the black areas on these aircraft gradually extended up the sides and over the fins and rudders. Many had Dull Red serials before this came about. In mid-1941 the norm for night bombers was Dark Green/Dark Earth/Special Night, with the latter terminating in a very wavy finish high on the fuselage and sweeping over the fins and rudders.

Blenheims of No 2 Group generally had Sky under surfaces by about May 1940 but during the Norwegian campaign a fair proportion still had black under surfaces. Their finish was amended in late August 1940 when Blenheims began night raids on barges and shipping gathering in the Channel ports for the invasion of Britain. These machines were hurriedly painted with removable black distemper on their under surfaces and on some it extended up their sides. Code letters remained medium grey, with black serials often being left on a rectangular panel of normal camouflage. White areas in national identity markings were sometimes painted over. Similar colours were applied to Blenheims of the Group during its night intruder activities in the winter of 1940/41.

In the spring and summer of 1941 No 2 Group devoted considerable effort to anti-shipping operations. By July some of its Blenheims had their upper surfaces and sides painted in the Temperate Sea Scheme, or had a dark grey shade in place of Dark Earth, possibly Dark Sea Grey.

Interdiction action against British bomber bases was at its greatest from late 1940 to mid-1941. The problems of camouflage when on the ground were therefore considered.

Black was long considered as an overall finish, but the bombers would have been conspicuous on the ground. It might have been good as night flying camouflage although trials suggested overall green was even better. The problems of painting all the night bombers caused the schemes to be dropped, although Whitleys operated in all-black finish between July 1941 and the end of that year.

High-altitude bombers brought problems. Fortress 1s originally had normal day bomber finish but in July 1941 some had Dark Earth replaced by a dark shade of grey and their under surfaces were repainted Azure Blue. Some Wellington VIs had Deep Sky under surfaces, and a few had theirs PRU Blue and their upper surfaces grey and green.

Stocks of Hall's Mid-Green Distemper were ordered in case night bombers were needed for daylight operations. One Stirling was flying in

Home-based bombers   15

this scheme in March 1942.

Mosquito bombers posed special problems. Originally they were finished Dark Green/Dark Earth/Sky with black spinners but this identified them too easily as bombers. Azure Blue under surfaces were considered but finally they operated in the same colours as day fighters with Sky codes, Sky spinners and yellow wing leading edge stripes. These latter and Sky trimmings were soon discarded because they made the aircraft too clearly visible on low level operations. Sky codes were retained to aid formating on day raids.

The rough finish of dope on bombers was a constant cause of complaint, particularly with the thick Special Night. A refinement came whereby the finish improved whilst reflectiveness was cut to a minimum. A smooth black dope came into general use in 1942, and was retained until the end of the war, but some machines were in use in 1943 with a very thin matt satin-like finish. As the war progressed the finish of the night dope became slightly more glossy, for it was found that this tended to bounce searchlight beams rather than enhance the presence of the aircraft. Searchlight defeat assumed less importance as radar-guided night fighters became the chief worry, so that speed gains were valuable. When Mosquitoes were switched to night bombing their under surfaces and sides were painted smooth black, the top edge of which was straight as it had been on many night bombers since 1942.

Whereas the purpose of squadron

Beaufort L4449 in early finish for the type, Dark Green/Dark Earth/silver with Type B roundels. The aircraft became OA:H of No 22 Squadron then passed to No 217 Squadron August 17 1940, staying till November 1940. Between July and November 1941 it was with No 86 Squadron. Later it served with the Torpedo Training Unit, 5 OTU, 2 TTU and 2 OTU before being SOC June 19 1945.

letters on fighters was to enable pilots to formate easily with other aircraft of the same squadron, bomber crews used theirs as radio call signs. Up to 1944 some bombers had a bar painted above their individual letters, believed to have been applied to the letters A, B, C, E, M, O, P and X. Another system was to use the 'squared' letter like A², B², etc. In May 1943 these aircraft were grouped in 'C' Flights, some of which were raised to squadron status. Others were given their own identity letters, so that No 7 Squadron for instance wore the codes MG as well as XU applied to Lancasters of 'C' Flight.

After the changes to Dull Red codes in May and new roundels in July 1942, bomber markings in the then-current styles were retained until the end of the war with few alterations. Some Mosquito IXs and XVIs had black under surfaces and tail areas, but most of the XVIs wore Dark Green/Ocean Grey/Medium Sea Grey finish. From about March 1943 Boston IIIs and, later, Mk IVs of No 2 Group were seen in American colours of Olive Drab/Neutral Grey or mixes of

RAF Camouflage of World War 2

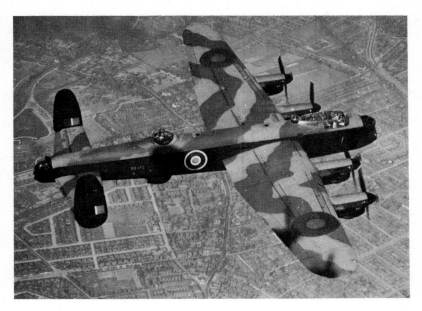

Lancaster RE172 exhibits typical Lancaster camouflage, although not all Lancasters had black lines above the wings. RE172 was later repainted in the 'Far East' black/white scheme for service in the Middle East at Fayid 1945-6.

Dark Green/Neutral Grey. Such schemes were also worn throughout their use by Mitchells whereas Venturas had a Dark Green/Dark Earth/Sky finish with Dull Red codes and serials like other day bombers.

Fighter-bomber Mosquito VIs were either Dark Green/Medium Sea Grey with the latter colour also on their under surfaces, or they had Ocean Grey as the upper grey colour, this being less common and intended for aircraft used on *Day Ranger* flights and intruder missions. Squadron letters on these Mosquitoes were Sky, and some had Sky spinners and a few

had Sky rear fuselage bands. Unarmed Mosquito T III trainers used by Mosquito fighter-bomber squadrons wore standard day fighter finish.

For night operations during which they provided bomber support, Mosquitoes had black under surfaces and sides, standard on 100 Group Mosquitoes from 1943 to 1945. Codes were Dull Red. Fortresses and Liberators of 100 Group wore standard night bomber finish, and exceptionally a few Fortresses were black overall. Codes on these aircraft were Dull Red, except for some in a training unit which carried yellow letters.

Home-based bombers

four

Coastal and photo recce aircraft

At the outbreak of war Coastal Command aircraft were mostly finished in the Temperate Land Scheme (Dark Green and Dark Earth) with silver under surfaces. Some aircraft retained black under surfaces from pre-war days. By late autumn 1939 silver under surfaces were usual, but some bomber aircraft temporarily with the Command, and the mine-busting Wellington DW aircraft, wore normal bomber camouflage.

The most startling breakaway in camouflage colouring was applied to the collection of aircraft used for the development of photo reconnaissance at PDU Heston. Operationally the unit relied upon Spitfires, Hudsons (P5139 and P5160) and Blenheim IVs. These it painted in somewhat bizarre schemes mostly relying upon the new greenish shade which became Sky and developing variations upon it. Some aircraft were painted overall in a pale colour,

others had it on their under sides.

By the spring of 1940 these aircraft were flying in assorted roundels, the pale green Blenheims, for example, having Type B above their wings and Type A on the fuselages. Some Spitfires had Type A above the wings and below with Type A on the fuselage.

An astonishing scheme was tried on a Hudson, consisting of duck egg green under surfaces with five duck egg green diagonal bands sloping from port to starboard across the entire upper surfaces and sides which were mottled dark green. It carried only Type B roundels.

The first change on General Reconnaissance aircraft came in June 1940 when Blenheim IV fighters acquired Sky under surfaces. Prior to this, Blenheim fighters introduced into the Command in February 1940 retained black and white under surfaces dating from their service with Fighter Command. Exceptionally, some had black under surfaces.

Since November 1939 GR aircraft had worn Type A roundels above their wings, some of which contained a narrow white ring. All were ordered to be changed to Type B from July 19 1940.

After service trials Liberator GR1 AM910 was passed to No 120 Squadron on September 5 1941 and served until March 1942. Finish here is Slate Grey and Extra Dark Sea Grey with Sky under surfaces (IWM).

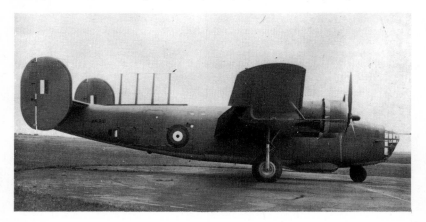

RAF Camouflage of World War 2

An exception to the normal Temperate Land Scheme for GR aircraft was slowly introduced from the autumn of 1939 whereby flying-boats, when beached for major overhaul — and beaching a boat and taking it into a hangar was indeed a major operation — were repainted in the Temperate Sea Scheme of Dark Slate Grey and Extra Dark Sea Grey, codes remaining medium grey. As in the case of GR landplanes, their under surfaces remained silver.

At an Air Ministry conference of July 4 1940 it was proposed that GR aircraft should have matt black under surfaces for night operations and Sky for day. Coastal Command pointed out that its squadrons — except for the Blenheim fighters — operated by day and night, and stated its preference for 75 per cent of its aircraft to have black and the remainder Sky. Mulling over the proposals Command signalled to Air Ministry on July 31 that all aircraft except Sunderlands should have Sky under surfaces, black distemper being

Liberators of No 120 Squadron at Aldergrove on April 10 1943 in Dark Slate Grey/Extra Dark Grey/white finish. Serials and codes are black. FK228:M nearest was used by the squadron from February 26 to September 12 1943 and in 1944-45 by No 1332 HCU. FL933:0 stands next in line and beyond a Mk V with chin radome (IWM).

applied prior to night operations. Although Sky and silver produced similar effects, Sky was considered better for camouflage purposes, and the aircraft were redoped this colour as they went in for major overhauls. Sunderlands, with silver under sides, did not even need Type A under wing roundels which were introduced on GR aircraft in July 1940, since they were so easy to identify.

In the case of some flying-boats and floatplanes it was necessary to define upper surfaces as those seen from above, fuselage sides and the fin and rudder. Upper surfaces of lower mainplanes and floats (excluding planing surfaces) were also to be considered as upper surfaces. Interplane struts of biplanes were to be considered as upper surfaces, but struts supporting floats were usually in under surface colours. Under surfaces of mainplanes would be in under surface colours. Orders now were that when upper and lower surface colours met they should be merged, forming no definite demarcation line. On August 23 1940 it was ordered that the under surfaces of all flying-boats were to become Sky.

An operational derivative of the PDU was formed as No 1 PRU at Heston. Its Spitfires wore mainly an overall pale shade of green or blue. When No 3 PRU formed at Oakington in Bomber Command it also acquired Spitfires in a variety of colours. Official records state that these latter aircraft wore

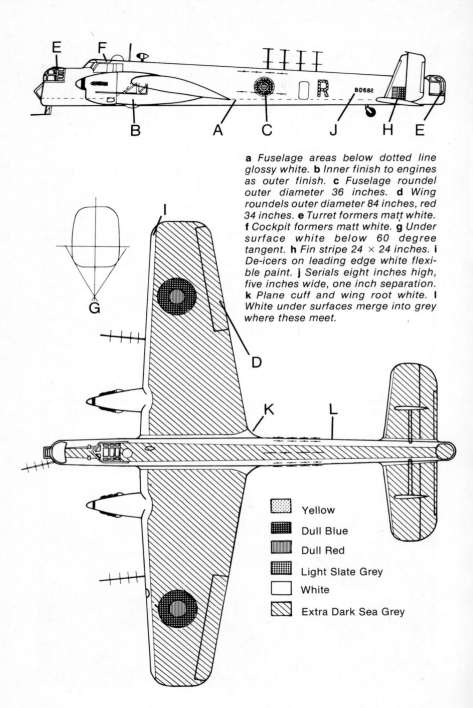

a *Fuselage areas below dotted line glossy white.* b *Inner finish to engines as outer finish.* c *Fuselage roundel outer diameter 36 inches.* d *Wing roundels outer diameter 84 inches, red 34 inches.* e *Turret formers matt white.* f *Cockpit formers matt white.* g *Under surface white below 60 degree tangent.* h *Fin stripe 24 × 24 inches.* i *De-icers on leading edge white flexible paint.* j *Serials eight inches high, five inches wide, one inch separation.* k *Plane cuff and wing root white.* l *White under surfaces merge into grey where these meet.*

Yellow
Dull Blue
Dull Red
Light Slate Grey
White
Extra Dark Sea Grey

standard colours, but this was not so. From observation it can be said that they wore an assortment of light colours — pale green, electric blue, matt white and even pink overall. The unit flew Wellington 1cs T2706 and T2707 in standard night bomber colours without codes.

During 1941 reconnaissance Spitfires gradually adopted a standard finish of PRU Blue with, in the case of No 1 PRU, LY codes in pale grey or matt white, serials being of the same shade. Roundels were now either Type A or B or a mixture with corresponding fin stripe colours. There never seemed to be much standardisation on these aircraft in 1941. Another variation existed in that some Spitfires had a very glossy finish. On others it was decidedly matt. Mosquitoes of No 1 PRU were PRU Blue overall, but a few had Dark Green/Ocean Grey finish with Medium Sea Grey under surfaces.

The question of whether Coastal Command land-based aircraft should have black or Sky under surfaces was subject to much discussion in the autumn of 1940. In September the Command considered that all should be black, and this would apply also to Beaufort torpedo bombers, hitherto

Armstrong-Whitworth Whitley GR Mk VII BD682 was delivered to No 32 MU on August 16 1942 and, after modification to operational needs at Hooton Park, joined No 612 Squadron in September 1942. It went to No 38 MU in July 1943 in the markings depicted and was finally scrapped at Cambridge. The drawing is based upon Armstrong-Whitworth diagram AW94741 dated March 1 1943. Upper surfaces of Extra Dark Sea Grey were painted in dope (ref DTD 308 – 33B/-225-227), the remainder of the machine being white-doped (ref DTD 308 – 33B/75, 76, 331). Serials and the identity letter were Light Slate Grey (ref DTD 308 – 33B/234, 236) and roundels were in yellow (DTD 308 – 33B/77, 78, 156), blue (DTD 308 – 33B/69, 70, 327), white (DTD 308 – 33B/75, 76, 331) and red (DTD 308 – 33B/73, 74, 330).

silver or Sky. Squadrons were unhappy about daylight strike missions in aircraft black underneath, and requested that such aircraft have Sky undersides. But the problem of maintaining aircraft specifically for day or night operations was too difficult to surmount. Meanwhile Ansons were still entering the Command with silver under surfaces as previously ordered, and were left in this finish and not painted black in case of allotment to other Commands who might want another change of finish.

Some Blenheim fighters received by the Command had black under surfaces during September, but squadrons were told that they were to revert to Sky with Type A underwing roundels. In October the Command requested that some aircraft be delivered ex-works in Sky finish instead of black, but alternative finishing on the lines was deemed impracticable. But black aircraft could not easily be overpainted Sky and it was then further decided to provide semi-permanent black paint to be applied over Sky. Trials flown from Thornaby with Hudsons having various upper surface colours proved how difficult it was to devise the ideal, but black under surfaces were at all times conspicuous by day.

A further conference held on October 28 1940 resolved the question of black versus Sky as follows: 25 per cent of GR and torpedo bomber landplanes would have Sky under surfaces and the remainder black; flying-boat under surfaces would be bare of any colour to allow cleaning of spray from hulls, then they would be covered with clear lanolin, reckoned to give the best protection against corrosion and allow early detection of it. Ordinary lanolin would later be tinted with Sky pigmentation currently under development.

In November upper surfaces of GR and torpedo bomber landplanes were still Temperate Land. Shorts tried out the use of all needed shades of camouflage paint made from a lanolin base. Bothas at No 3 School of GR in December 1940 were painted with Sky under surfaces since they flew by day.

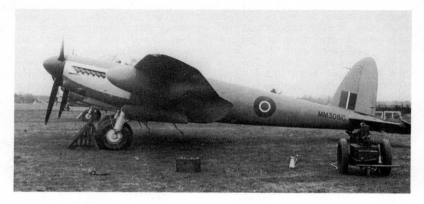

Beaufighters now being introduced also wore Temperate Land Scheme with Sky under surfaces.

Aircraft in the Coastal Operational Training Units posed some problems. Ansons and Oxfords had either yellow or Sky under sides when it was standard practice for all OTU aircraft to wear operational colours, although many Ansons in bomber OTUs still wore yellow under surfaces. In Coastal Command the usual policy was agreed whereby Ansons and Oxfords would wear Sky under surfaces and any aircraft used for target towing would have yellow and black striped under sides. When Whitleys and Wellingtons first entered the Command they did so in Temperate Land Scheme with black under surfaces and sides, but these were soon changed to Sky on the relatively small numbers received.

In July 1941 the prescribed colours for Coastal Command aircraft were: operational landplanes — Temperate Sea Scheme with mainly black and some Sky under surfaces; flying-boats — Temperate Sea Scheme of Dark Slate Grey and Extra Dark Sea Grey with Sky pigmented under surfaces.

By 1941 Coastal Command was vigorously engaged in the anti-U-boat war, and trials that year were undertaken to discover the most effective colour scheme for aircraft when attacking submarines. A surprising scheme was devised whereby the under sides, fins and rudders of aircraft would be white to give them best

There were anomalies in roundel types on PR aircraft throughout the war, as seen here on Mosquito MM308/G shortly before it was passed to the USAF for H2X trials. Overall finish was PR Blue.

Short Sunderland Mk 1 P9601 was delivered to Pembroke Dock November 3 1939 and joined No 10 Squadron, Royal Australian Air Force, at the end of the month. It moved to Mount Batten with the squadron on April 1 1940 where it was burnt out in a hangar as a result of an air raid on Plymouth on the night of November 27/28 1940. The drawing is based upon Short Bros diagram S25C 29103 of June 14 1940. The camouflage markings shown were applicable to Sunderlands N9027, '029, '044, '046, '048, '050, P0601, '603, '605, '620, '622, '624, T9041, '043, '045, '047, '049, T9070, '072, '074, '076 and '078. All of these wore Scheme 'B' which was applied to alternately built aircraft and not necessarily those with odd number serials. Intervening machines wore the mirror image camouflage pattern. Paints used were to specification DTD 308 and 314 for metal surfaces, DTD 83 for fabric covered surfaces. The initial camouflage scheme for the Sunderland was prescribed on June 20 1939 and subsequent alterations were dated November 3 1939, March 2 1940 and June 14 1940. A further revision of the period came on December 16 1940.

RAF Camouflage of World War 2

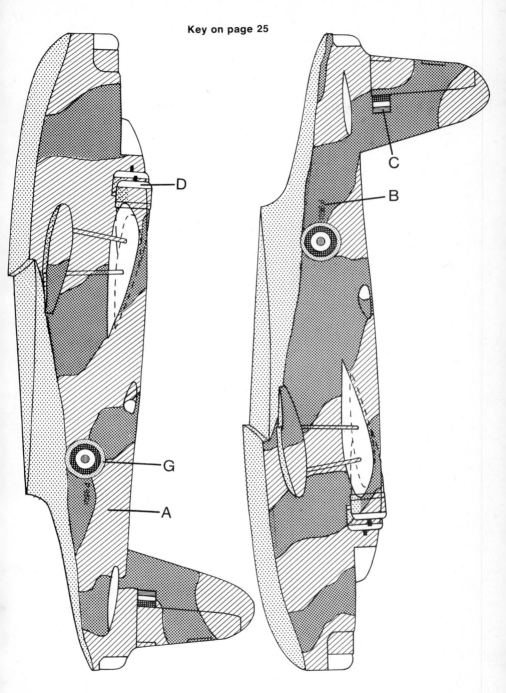

Coastal and photo recce aircraft

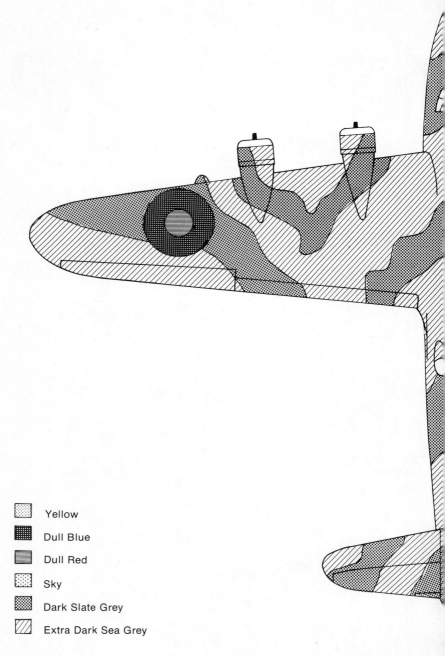

Yellow

Dull Blue

Dull Red

Sky

Dark Slate Grey

Extra Dark Sea Grey

RAF Camouflage of World War 2

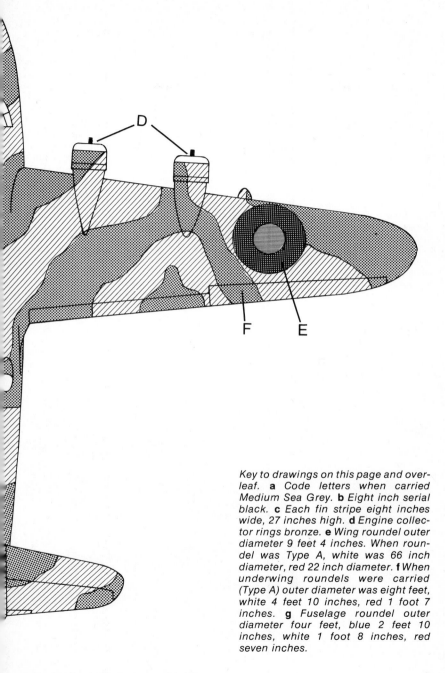

Key to drawings on this page and over-leaf. **a** Code letters when carried Medium Sea Grey. **b** Eight inch serial black. **c** Each fin stripe eight inches wide, 27 inches high. **d** Engine collector rings bronze. **e** Wing roundel outer diameter 9 feet 4 inches. When roundel was Type A, white was 66 inch diameter, red 22 inch diameter. **f** When underwing roundels were carried (Type A) outer diameter was eight feet, white 4 feet 10 inches, red 1 foot 7 inches. **g** Fuselage roundel outer diameter four feet, blue 2 feet 10 inches, white 1 foot 8 inches, red seven inches.

cover when engaged by anti-aircraft fire when they were flying against a grey sky. First orders to paint the aircraft in this striking finish were given in August 1941 and they applied to Wellingtons, Whitleys and flying boats whilst Beauforts, Beaufighters, Blenheims and Hudsons acquired the newly authorised Temperate Sea Scheme with Sky under surfaces.

On August 10 1941 the camouflage for the large aircraft was further prescribed as sides (surfaces visible from eight degrees or more below the horizontal) being matt white and under surfaces (ie those seen from directly below) glossy white. The remaining upper surfaces were to be in the Temperate Sea Scheme. Under surfaces of torpedo bombers and long range fighters would be 50 per cent black and the rest Sky. In the case of the large aircraft the re-painting would take place over a long period.

Painting orders of August 6 1941 specified painting the large aircraft glossy white (DTD 260A/33b 161) on their under surfaces and matt white (Stores Reference 33b/168/169) on their sides which merged with the upper surface colours at the datum line. Sides of fins and rudders would be matt white. De-icing boots on lead-ing edges were ordered to be painted with a special flexible white paint — hitherto they had been black. Cowlings would be painted with white stoving enamel.

The two basic schemes of Temperate Sea/Sky and Temperate Sea/white were prevalent in 1942 with squadron codes being Medium Sea Grey on the former and usually Dark Slate Grey on the latter which had the customary eight-inch serials in the same colour. Some variations in code colours were recorded, with aircraft bearing Dull Red letters and even black letters and serials.

Coastal Command Ansons in the summer of 1940 retaining the white area in upper wing roundels. K6285 nearest first served with No 224 Squadron and joined No 217 Squadron in June 1939. It passed to Station Flight Carew Cheriton on July 21 1940 and is seen here in their hands still coded MW:F. On the fin is the yellow triangle outlined black carried by aircraft of the Netherlands Naval Air Service. N9742 in the distance also has this and at the time the photograph was taken was being flown by No 321 Squadron (IWM).

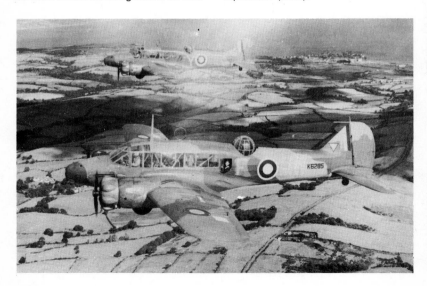

Top *Beaufort W6498:AW-K of 42 Squadron in Slate Grey and Extra Dark Sea Grey with black under surfaces for night operations. Code letters look to be white with 'Killer' on the nose in red. Used by No 42 Squadron May 30 to September 29 1941, and later by Nos 143 and 217 Squadrons and 9 OTU.* **Above** *A typical high-altitude reconnaissance aircraft is seen here, Spitfire PRXI, EN654. Overall finish is PR Blue with a grey serial. All roundels are Type B. EN654 joined No 16 Squadron in October 1943 after flying on development work. After the war it flew with Fighter Command Communication Squadron from Northolt.*

In January 1943 a further revision of colours for large aircraft took place, as a result of which the entire upper surfaces became Extra Dark Sea Grey, which colour also applied to Halifaxes from their introduction into the Command.

So successful was the white finish that in January 1943 it was recommended for all Coastal Command aircraft. In the case of flying-boats the hull and float planing bottoms were coated with anti-fouling paint DTD 420B/33b 37 over which was applied a coating of DTD420B 33b/463. Wing and tailplane under surfaces became glossy as a result of the application of three coats of DTD 420/33b 463.

The upper limit of the white areas had nullified the effectiveness of the two-tone camouflage and painting them Extra Dark Sea Grey only also

cut man hours. Insides of fins and rudders were still white and some wing leading edge de-icers would now be silver. Code letters were still to be Slate Grey. The white/grey finish also applied to aircraft operating in a maritime role overseas, but many of them throughout their careers retained two-tone upper surfaces. Coastal Command still wanted some aircraft with black under surfaces. Overseas these were mainly the torpedo bomber Wellingtons in the Middle East. At home they were mainly Albacores and Swordfish of 119 Squadron which retained two-tone upper surfaces or were black overall.

The white areas later defined as those which would be seen from the front or side elevation were retained until the end of the war. The white on engine nacelles was applied upwards

Coastal and photo recce aircraft

A Beaufighter VIC in standard mid-war two-tone coastal camouflage with the 1943 style of Coastal coding, in this case '2-G' in red outlined white. Nose ASV has been deleted by the censor.

to cover the whole top surfaces forward of the boundary of the upper surface colouring of the wing near the leading edge. Flame damping exhausts were painted in white anti-glow paint. A second method of obtaining the ordered gloss finish on under surfaces was by a finish of transparent dope and a third by the use of synthetic white DTD 260A.

Coastal Command had Medium Grey codes until the introduction of the white finish when letters and serials were ordered to be Slate Grey. Some units, however, chose Dull Red. For some months in 1943, for security reasons, flying-boats and land planes of the Command were given a new code-letter system whereby each station used a single digit number to identify each of its squadrons, so that in place of the usual two-letter codes the observer saw 1:A, 1:B, 2:A, 2:B, etc, the letter identifying the aircraft.

This was a confusing system preventing any identity of the aircraft's unit except by serial number. It remained in use on some machines until 1944, and some Coastal OTUs operated the system for many months. When it was discontinued quite a lot of the squadrons adopted new identity letters. In June 1943 some Beaufighters received Dull Red codes, kept until about mid-1944, then their letters were often Sky, although some squadrons retained red to the end of the war. The white scheme was authorised

for Beaufighters in March 1943, and also for ASR Warwicks, many of which operated with Slate Grey and Extra Dark Sea Grey upper surfaces. Mks II and V were all painted in the white/grey scheme. Some Hampden and Beaufort torpedo bombers in use in 1943 had white formation stripes painted on their wing upper surfaces along the centre of the wing from root to tip and, used in conjunction with Clouston formation-keeping lights, they enabled loose formation night flying.

Torpedo bombers went through the same marking stages as other types, viz: Temperate Land Scheme/Sky, Temperate Sea Scheme/Sky or black, Temperate Sea Scheme/white and Extra Dark Sea Grey/white. The Beaufort had been phased out before the latter scheme came into play although some late production Beauforts and some used for training wore the scheme. Some Hampdens wore it. Their replacement type was the Beaufighter which served mainly in Temperate Sea Scheme/Sky and from November 1943 in Extra Dark Sea Grey/Sky with black, Sky or Dull Red codes. For a short time some Beaufighter torpedo bombers had Dark Sea Grey sides.

When Coastal Command began to use Mosquito FB VIs in some numbers their usual finish was Temperate Sea with Sky under surfaces, but some wore Extra Dark Sea Grey during the

RAF Camouflage of World War 2

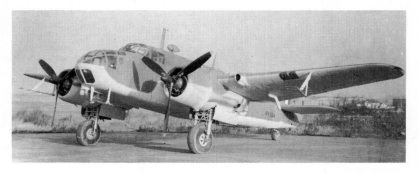

Top *Beaufort AW304 in Dark Slate Grey/Extra Dark Sea Grey finish.* **Above** *A 1943 photograph of Lysander BA:E in air-sea rescue service with Temperate Sea Scheme and Sky under surfaces. Codes red* (IWM).

later period of service. Mosquito codes varied in colour through Sky to black outlined white and to Dull Red. When AEAF stripes were applied to the attack squadron aircraft the Sky or Dull Red codes were often placed entirely forward of the fuselage roundels with a hyphen separating the unit letters from the individual letter.

From 1942 until the end of the war photo reconnaissance aircraft wore PR Blue (renamed such in February 1942) with Type B wing roundels on upper surfaces and Type B or C fuselage roundels and fin flashes. From April 1944 PR Mosquitoes were ordered to have Type B roundels. In the 2nd TAF some Spitfires had an assortment of Type C1 roundels.

By 1945 there were still variations in aircraft colouring. Code letters on large aircraft were now often black, the colours varying from station to station, and this was also true of the colours of serials. Many aircraft finished the war still in Temperate Sea Scheme/white and in the case of Liberators they continued to wear this even when serving in Transport Command during 1945 and 1946.

Coastal and photo recce aircraft

five

Transport aircraft

Apart from a handful of Bristol Bombays the only RAF transport aircraft in September 1939 were small machines used for communications duties, such as Vega Gulls, DH 86s and DH 89s. Before camouflage had come into general use these aircraft were all silver with black serials. Then they flew with Dark Green and Dark Earth upper surfaces whilst their undersides remained silver. A few were seen with black/white under surfaces in the manner of fighters, but on the outbreak of war a standard finish of Dark Green and Dark Earth with yellow under surfaces came into play. A feature which generally distinguished transports from trainers was the absence of under wing serials, although some trainers switched to a transport role retained serials.

The ranks of the transport force were swelled by the large scale requisition of a wide assortment of civil aircraft impressed into RAF service. Such machines wore the Dark Green/Dark Earth/yellow scheme to the end of the war and many were used as light transports, squadron hacks, etc.

In August 1940 the order was given that troop carriers and bomber transports would acquire Sky under surfaces and to the end of that year the under surface colouring came half way up the fuselage sides. Very few aircraft were involved — mainly Bombays. Squadron letters were not carried.

Late in 1940 upper surface colours were again extended to the base of the fuselage.

The first new British transport to be

introduced was the Armstrong-Whitworth Albemarle, transferred from its unhappy career as a bomber. It entered service as a transport with No 511 Squadron at Lyneham in February 1943. Their aircraft, used between Britain and the Middle East, had Dark Green/Dark Earth/Azure Blue finish. Individual letters were Dull Red, but they carried no squadron code. At Lyneham the Albemarles joined a collection of Liberators of No 1425 Flight which were already finished in the

Avro York C Mk 1 MW101 was delivered in the colours depicted to No 511 Squadron at Lyneham on November 13 1943 for use of the Chief of the Air Staff. It was transferred to No 24 Squadron based at Northolt on February 28 1944 and to the Metropolitan Communications Squadron on September 23 1944. Subsequently No 246 Squadron used the machine which was with No 511 Squadron again by the end of 1945. In March 1946, now in silver finish it joined No 1359 VIP Flight at Bassingbourn with whom it operated until mid-January 1948 when it again joined No 24 Squadron. The Far East Communications Squadron acquired the aircraft in January 1951. It returned to Britain the following September and was scrapped at No 22 MU in June 1955. The drawing depicts the finish applied to early production Yorks from the end of 1943, the depicted scheme being in vogue well into 1946.

a Centre fin pattern same as fin face, inner fin faces as for outer pattern on opposite fin. b Black fuselage serials eight inches high, five wide, one inch spacing. c Upper wing roundel centred 10 feet 8½ inches from tip. d Roundel outer diameter 8 feet 4 inches. e Fuselage roundel outer diameter 54 inches. f Underwing roundel Type C, outer diameter 48 inches. g Fin stripe 17 inches — two inches — 17 inches, 24 inches high. h Position of underwing roundel indicated in red area. i Some aircraft had camouflaged top to tail cone, also Azure extending to tip of nose.

RAF Camouflage of World War 2

Please
affix
stamp of
correct
value

HAESSNER PUBLISHING, INC.
DRAWER B
NEWFOUNDLAND, N.J. 07435

HAESSNER PUBLISHING, INC.
DRAWER B
NEWFOUNDLAND, N.J. 07435

Publishers and distributors of specialised quality books

We hope you will enjoy reading this book. To help us ensure that we publish books of real interest on specialised subjects, we would be grateful if you would complete this short questionnaire and drop it in the nearest post box. With this guidance, we will keep you informed of our future publishing plans and you may then order further books from your bookseller or if you have difficulty in obtaining them by that method, direct from us through the post. If you are already on our regular mailing list or if you have previously completed and returned one of these cards, there is no need to send another. Please write below the title of the book from which you obtained this post card.

Book Title _____

Block capitals please

Name _____

Address _____

_____

1 How did you obtain this book?

□□□□

PURCHASED FROM BOOKSELLER
PURCHASED BY MAIL ORDER
PURCHASED ELSEWHERE
RECEIVED AS A PRESENT

2 In which other sports, hobbies or pastimes are you interested?

□□□□□□□□□□□□□□□□

AIRCRAFT
FINE ART
HANDICRAFTS
MILITARY SUBJECTS
MODEL MAKING
MOTORCYCLING
MOTORING AND MOTOR RACING
NATURAL HISTORY
PHOTOGRAPHY
RAILWAYS
SHIPS
SUPERNATURAL
TRAVEL
WARGAMING
YACHTING AND SMALL BOATS
OTHER INTERESTS _____

3 If you would like a copy of our current catalogue, please tick this box □

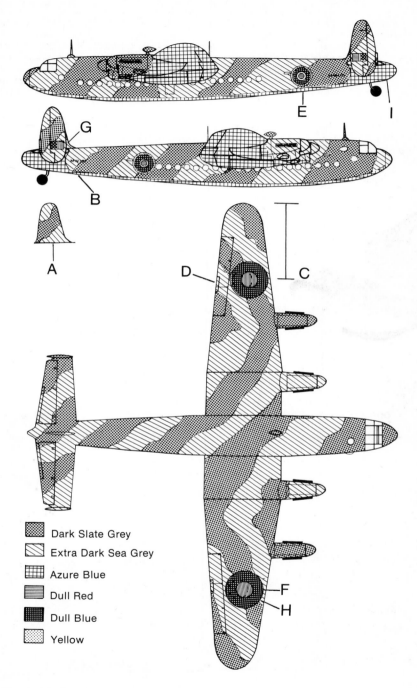

Dark Slate Grey

Extra Dark Sea Grey

Azure Blue

Dull Red

Dull Blue

Yellow

Transport aircraft

Temperate Sea Scheme with Azure Blue under surfaces, a scheme also applied to some Albemarles since much of their flying was over the sea. Type C1 roundels were painted on their fuselages, Type B above the wing tips and some had Type C beneath the wing tips.

In addition to the afore-mentioned Liberators, there were those of the Atlantic Ferry Return Organisation which operated out of Prestwick. Its aircraft had bomber camouflage with red serials. Their ownership was complicated in as much as some in RAF markings were flown by BOAC crews. By the end of the war some of these Liberators were flying in natural finish, a special example of which was the famous 'Commando', AL504. The few Liberator IXs used, distinctive with a huge fin and rudder, also had natural finish.

On May 18 1943 an order was issued that all production transport aircraft operating to destinations outside of the UK would be finished (and retrospectively painted) in a Temperate Sea Scheme with Azure Blue under surfaces. By mid-1943 the transport Albemarles were in a variety of schemes — Temperate Land with Azure Blue or Sky under surfaces and Temperate Sea with Azure Blue under surfaces. None carried squadron let-

ters but individual letters in Dull Red or Sky were still worn by some.

A decision that the Albemarle would serve as a glider tug/paratrooper whilst retaining a capability for bombing and supply dropping resulted in most being delivered in standard bomber camouflage of Dark Green, Dark Earth and black with red serials and later red codes. There was an interim period between late 1943 and about April 1944 when Albemarle glider tugs wore duplicated individual letters for identity applied either in white, light blue or red, colours varying among units.

In 1944 Halifax Vs entered service with airborne squadrons and also had double letter individual identities in Dull Red. Squadron coding later followed on the standard bomber camouflage.

The brunt of transport operations came to be borne by Dakotas, the first of which came into use in 1943. They were initially supplied in American colours, Olive Drab and Neutral Grey. Accidents and subsequent re-painting meant that some acquired similar British colours. There was no consistency in code letter colours, but usually they were Dull Red and sometimes Sky, white or even yellow. Individual letters were sometimes painted on the tip of the nose, or on the nose sides.

Bristol Buckinghams were mainly built as bombers, but their final purpose was as courier aircraft. This superseded plans to use them for GR work as Wellington replacements in the Middle East. Their finish was Dark Green/Dark Earth/Azure Blue. KV370 seen here has been modified into a transport.

Bombay transports home-based in the summer of 1940 had their Sky under surfaces partly up the fuselage sides. The aircraft belongs to No 271 Squadron (P. Scott).

Dakotas of No 575 Squadron Broadwell. Finish was Olive Drab/Neutral Grey with black serials and red codes outlined yellow. 19:A-FZ695 nearest arrived in Britain in February 1944 and was used by the squadron between April 1944 and December 1945. It later went to Canada (IWM).

Serial numbers were black. Usually the roundel separated unit from individual code letters, but some aircraft had these grouped together. Dakotas had Type C roundels under their wing tips, usually small.

A regular sight in many parts of Britain from 1941 onwards were Harrow bombers performing in a transport role, some with their turrets removed being known as 'Sparrows'. In 1941-43 these aircraft had Dark Green/Dark Earth/yellow finish like communications aircraft, and were used mainly to assist in squadron moves. In 1944 some of these aircraft were earmarked for a casevac role as a consequence of which they adopted a Temperate Sea Scheme finish with Azure Blue under surfaces. Code letters on these were Dull Red. They commuted between Britain and the continent after the invasion but at no time did they carry ambulance markings.

Ambulance aircraft were always few in number and in 1940 they were Dark Earth/Dark Green with white undersurfaces. On the fuselage side they carried a Red Cross sign on a white disc, repeated on the wings. Variations in the positioning of the ambulance marking occurred and it was chiefly applied for use in North Africa during the desert campaign.

It was in 1944 that the Stirling IV came into its own as a glider tug and paratrooper. These aircraft wore standard bomber camouflage with red codes and serials. The Stirling C V, intended for trooping in the Far East, began to be delivered to home bases in September 1944 in a Temperate Sea Scheme with Azure under surfaces. Squadron codes and serials were Dull Red or black. After the war many Stirlings Vs were used in natural finish, painted silver. These wore black codes and serials along with the special nose

Transport aircraft

Avro York G-AGJA of BOAC in late war civil camouflage with lettering underlined. Under surfaces are black.

identity codes which Transport Command relied upon as call signs.

The final transport type introduced during the war was the Avro York which saw only limited war service. Early machines were completed in Temperate Sea Scheme/Azure Blue with black serials. Silver Yorks belonged to post-war days like the silver Liberators pressed into service as transports when the war ended. Some Liberator transports retained American camouflage held during their service overseas and many had Coastal Command camouflage which included the two-tone style. Codes were white on the camouflaged bombers, black on silver aircraft and those retaining Coastal Command colours.

A group of aircraft that were a daily sight all over Britain during the war were the taxi aircraft of the Air Transport Auxiliary. A considerable number of Fairchild Argus light transports were used, entering use in 1941. To the end of their service these aircraft were finished in Dark Green/Dark Earth/yellow without individual identity, although the ATA often pressed for such.

six

Army co-operation aircraft

At the start of the war there were two types of army co-operation aircraft in use. Westland Lysanders were sent to France finished in Dark Green/Dark Earth with silver undersides. The Dark Green/Dark Earth camouflage covered the entire fuselage including its under surfaces.

Before the outbreak of hostilities Lysanders had worn black/white under surfaces because they were under Fighter Command's control, and some home-based Lysanders and Hectors retained such markings to late 1939. The Hector biplanes, whose markings were brought into line with the Lysanders in France, formed a small second line force ready to help if

ever needed.

French-based Lysanders operated closely with the army during May 1940 in the colours previously worn, and upon which squadron codes were Medium Grey. Those that struggled home were repainted in July and August to have Sky under surfaces first seen on the type in May 1940. Hectors already had this feature when they briefly operated in support of the Calais garrison before retiring from operational service.

At dawn and sunset for the rest of 1940 Lysanders were employed on East and South coast patrols, searching for evidence of German invaders. Basic colouring was unchanged, but their grey codes varied much in size and style, and some roundels were extremely large — presumably to give them added protection against 'trigger happy' army and naval gunners along the coastal regions.

Fighting in France showed the Lysander too big, too slow and too vulnerable for army support 1940 style. No replacement type came to hand until the Curtiss Tomahawk proved itself useless to Fighter Command. As a result many Tomahawks were turned over to Army Co-

A very rare shot indeed of a Stampe SV4B used by Captain Donnet in his escape from Belgium, subject of a recent book. Its normal communications aircraft finish is evident but the serial J7777 is ingenious and also appeared on the under surfaces of the aircraft which, for a time, also carried a serial in the V range. Photographed July 9 1942.

*An army co-opera-
tion Lysander
L4786:HB-U of 239
Squadron with
which it served
between September
1940 and April 1941
after service with
No 16 Squadron. It
was later used in
India (via J. Robert-
son).*

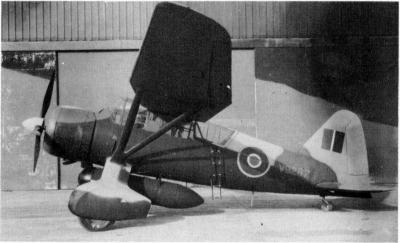

operation Command to supplement or
re-equip the Lysander squadrons from
early 1941.

There was some confusion over
their markings. Were they fighters or
not? As a result some Tomahawks
were flying in the first weeks of 1941
with half black under surfaces whilst
others remained all Sky. Two distinct
shades of Sky were visible on them,
one a rich Duck Egg Green shade, the
other a very blue tone. Sky spinners
and tail bands in fighter style were
gradually added to the Tomahawks
whose upper surfaces were Dark
Green and Dark Earth. Squadron
codes were medium grey. Spinners
had initially been black.

What was needed was a light, man-
oeuvrable liaison aircraft which could

*Lysanders used for special operations
work initially wore Dark Green/Dark
Earth/Sky finish. By 1943 Medium
Sea Grey had replaced Dark Earth and
under surfaces had become black as
shown. MA coding of No 161 Squadron
was red. This squadron sometimes
borrowed aircraft from army co-
operation units and even operated
aircraft in full target-towing colours.*

fly low, spot for guns and generally
report in safety using woodland and
the terrain for protection. It was found,
first in the Taylorcraft Plus Model D,
trials of which began in October 1939,
and then in its derivative the Auster
AOP 1. The experimental Taylorcraft
had silver under surfaces, then came

RAF Camouflage of World War 2

early production Auster 1s with yellow under surfaces, some of which were used to form the first squadron, No 651, in the summer of 1941. In 1942 an overall Dark Green/Dark Earth finish was adopted for AOP aircraft and retained to the end of the war, but overseas some AOPs had the two-tone brown scheme. Type B roundels were worn below and above the wings with Type C1 on the fuselage. Serials were black, code letters Sky, medium grey or red.

Blenheim bombers also operated during 1941-42 in a close support role with the Command. These were finished in Temperate Land/Sky with Medium Grey codes.

Lysander camouflage was unaltered in 1941-42 although some machines had their individual letter repeated black under the port wing tip to aid in reporting activities.

In the autumn of 1941 Tomahawks flew small scale *rhubarb* operations during which they photographed and shot up targets on the enemy coast. To afford maximum protection the Tomahawks were repainted in the then-standard Fighter Command Dark Green/Ocean Grey/Medium Grey/Sky scheme.

The closing weeks of 1942 saw the arrival of the North American Mustang. Again destined for Fighter Command, it was found to have a poor performance at high levels, but it performed excellently at low altitudes. During early spring 1942 it began to replace the Tomahawk, examples of the latter type thrown up by squadron conversion being used to form new army co-operation squadrons. Hurricanes in standard fighter colours supplemented the fighter reconnaissance force. Mustangs initially came into service in Dark Green/Dark Earth/Sky finish with black spinners and Medium Grey code letters.

Official instructions of July 1 1942 ordered that the Mustangs be repainted Ocean Grey/Dark Green/Medium Sea Grey with yellow outer wing leading edges. Codes would now be Sky, and the usual Sky trim was applied. Since the Mustang so resembled the Messerschmitt Bf 109 a one foot wide yellow band was ordered to be painted chordwise around each mainplane immediately outboard of the flaps. A few Mustangs had two of these bands around each wing, such as were worn by some Typhoons. Their value was partly nullified since they rendered the aircraft clear to enemy fighters both during combat and as they flew low-level paired patrols over enemy territory. The bands were removed in December 1942.

At the start of July, remaining Tomahawks in Army Co-operation Command were ordered to be finished in Ocean Grey/Dark Green/Medium Grey finish which hitherto had only been worn by those being used on offensive operations, to which use a few Mustangs had been put. The Tomahawk's days in the Command were almost over, after which they served at OTUs or in Bomber Defence Training Flights in standard fighter markings, often with red codes.

Whereas Fighter Command squadrons relied upon squadron codes when rallying after combat, paired Mustangs had no such need. Resulting from a Command idea, squadron letters were removed from Mustangs in March 1943 before Exercise 'Spartan' in which they were very actively engaged. Some Mustangs wore black distemper under surfaces and white stripes along the forward fuselage during the Exercise. These special markings were also applied to some other fighters.

Mustang 1s, 1As and IIs were employed in a fighter recce role to the end of the war, and between 1943 and 1945 retained their fighter finish with a Sky individual letter only and black serials.

The delimitation between army co-operation aircraft, tactical fighters and tactical fighter bombers vanished when Fighter Command took over Army Co-operation Command and later dissolved the tactical force into the 2nd TAF. In any case, from July 1942 the colours of the fighter recce force had become those of Fighter Command.

Army co-operation aircraft

seven

Trainers

Yellow as a colour for trainer aircraft was adopted in July 1936. Trials with a Tutor had revealed that a yellow aircraft was more easily visible than one of any other shade. The desire to warn pilots that training was taking place prompted the use of the overall yellow finish. Cowlings remained unpainted burnished metal.

Closeness of war in 1938 altered that scheme since yellow aircraft were easily visible on the ground. From the Munich crisis training aircraft had upper surfaces of wings, tailplane and fuselage camouflaged Dark Green and Dark Earth. The fuselage sides to about three-quarters of the way up were left yellow, likewise the wing under surfaces, top and bottom. Interplane struts were camouflaged, usually in one shade. To improve the camouflage effect on biplanes, par-ticularly when shadows of the upper main plane were cast across the lower, the latter were later coloured light Green and Light Earth although this is believed not to have come in until about April 1940. Black serials were displayed under the wings, on the rear fuselage and usually on the rudder which, like the fin, was painted yellow. Individual identity markings on trainers were usually black at this stage, but some had red before the war and during its early stages.

These markings also applied to Reserve and Service Flying Training School aircraft. By 1939, however, both regular and reserve formations were receiving Ansons and Battles, also employed in operational roles. These retained bomber camouflage and generally had yellow individual identity markings with white underwing serials. It was intended that they should have yellow under surfaces by mid-1939 — although this never came about — and that future examples for training purposes would have yellow finish.

Mid-placed in the training organisation were the Group Pools, forerunners of the Operational Training

Miles Magisters of No 15 EFTS in the summer of 1940. Note the yellow under surfaces extending up the fuselage sides. (C. Nepean Bishop).

Tiger Moth DF184:G has the yellow bars applied to trainers early 1944. These it wore during service with No 5 and later No 1 GTS.

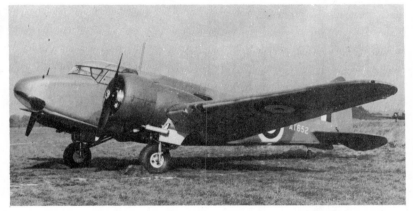

Airspeed Oxford AT652 in 1941 style trainer colours has a yellow fuselage serial. Note how the fuselage serial reaches the base of the fuselage. After service with 7 BAT Flight it passed to 1507 BAT Flight, 1516 BAT Flight and to 1382 Transport Support Conversion unit in 1946. Photographed October 22 1941.

Units which were first formed in April 1940. Aircraft in Pools, which had operational commitments, wore standard camouflage of their operational equivalents and the squadron letters of the units from which they had formed, or were unmarked in any special way in the case of the Fighter Group Pools. A suggestion at one time that operational types of aircraft used for training should have black/white under surfaces was never followed up.

In April 1940 the fins and rudders of trainers were all ordered to be camouflaged. Rudder serials were not reinstated. In May 1940 trainers were ordered to have fin stripes applied. Underwing roundels were not made mandatory until May 1940, but many aircraft carried them before this date and some had always worn them. On August 1 1940 orders were given that yellow under surfaces would apply to trainers and additionally to the aircraft of the School of Army Co-operation, the Autogiro Training Flight, Torpedo Training Unit, Torpedo Development Unit and the Seaplane Training Squadron.

On November 7 1940 an instruction was given that upper camouflage on all training aircraft would extend down to the base of the fuselage, making the aircraft less conspicuous on the

Trainers

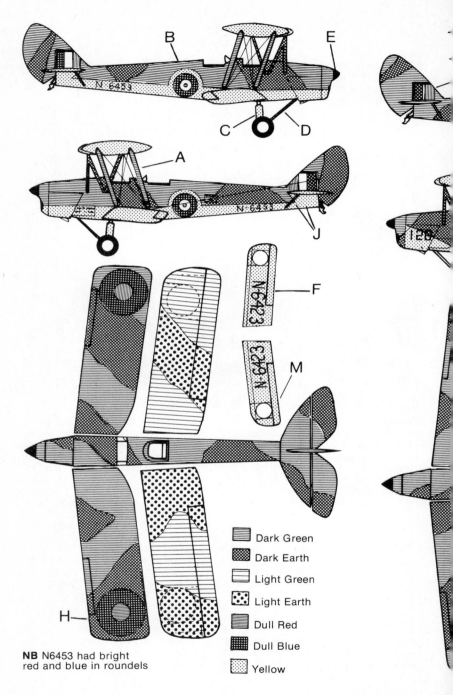

Dark Green

Dark Earth

Light Green

Light Earth

Dull Red

Dull Blue

Yellow

NB N6453 had bright red and blue in roundels

RAF Camouflage of World War 2

De Havilland Tiger Moth N6453, wearing the 'B' Scheme as applied to Tiger Moths with odd numbered serials, carries the markings worn by Tiger Moths in Training Command in mid-1940. The machine was initially delivered to No 34 E & R FTS in January 1938. 'A' and 'B' Schemes were applied to Tiger Moths to about T7341, after which all were finished in the 'A' Scheme on the production lines, although for a considerable time the two schemes remained in evidence until re-spraying took place at MUs, etc. The illustration is based on DH Drawing No M6424. Notes on the drawing state that fin stripes (mod 10854) were added May 22 1940, roundels were added on under surfaces May 28 1940 (mod 10860), but they were deleted on August 22 then re-applied August 28 1940. Typical underwing serial and roundel position is shown on the original drawing on a fictitious N6423.

De Havilland Tiger Moth T5888 wears the 'A' Scheme and is depicted as recorded at 22 EFTS in November 1943. Mod 14070 resulted in 'C Type' roundels, ordered on May 21 1942. T5888 was initially delivered to 39 MU on July 31 1940 and joined 22 EFTS on December 11 1940 where it stayed until passed to 6 EFTS June 2 1944. 38 MU received the machine August 21 1946 and it was used at the Blind Landing Experimental Unit post-war. T7022 was used by No 22 EFTS between January 22 1941 and July 30 1945 and was recorded in the markings shown in January 1944. The top illustration of a typical Tiger Moth fuselage of mid-1944 shows the yellow bar markings. Two upper wing tip yellow areas are shown, the top being that as worn at 22 EFTS at the end of 1943, whereby the extreme wing tips were outlined yellow. The lower wing tip is shown bearing a four foot yellow area as standard from about June 1944 at 22 EFTS.

a Interplane struts all Dark Green. **b** Four inch wide band around fuselage roundels. **c** Chassis, underside of wings, tailplane and petrol tank yellow

DTD 145. **d** *Undercarriage radius rods Dark Earth.* **e** *Front and rear faces of propeller matt black, yellow four inches from tip.* **f** *Position of underwing black serials, two feet high and ten inches wide with five inch spacing.* **g** *Underwing roundel Type C 16 inches in outer diameter.* **h** *Upper wing roundel, blue diameter 3 feet 8 inches, red 1 foot 5 inches.* **i** *Fuselage roundel Type C1, outer diameter 18 inches, blue 16 inches, white eight inches, red six inches.* **j** *Tailplane stay Dark Green.* **k** *Fin stripes eight inches — two inches — eight inches, and extend to rudder.* **l** *All camouflage to extend over wing and tail leading edges to ensure no yellow is visible from above.* **m** *Underwing roundels sited between second and fourth ribs.* **n** *Scheme 'A'.* **o** *Scheme 'B'.* **p** *Interim yellow wing tip.* **q** *Later standard yellow wing tip.* **r** *Yellow strips flanking roundel 1944 style.*

ground. The alteration took place in the closing weeks of 1940, setting the basic scheme for home-based trainers to the end of the war. Overseas — in Canada, Africa and Australia — where the Empire Air Training Scheme was now fully underway — the aircraft were yellow overall with black or red lettering, which scheme was retained in these zones to the close of hostilities.

Black did not show much against the camouflage so Sky or Training Yellow identity numbers/letters were now painted on home-based trainers. This was a minor identity feature when applied to trainers, for it was almost an unbroken rule that they carried their serial number in black on the under surfaces whereas identical types of aircraft used for communications purposes generally had no underwing serials. Wing serials were used to identify the aircraft by instructors and were also useful in discouraging young, exuberant pilots from low flying.

Inevitably, when training types passed to other units as 'hack' aircraft for many purposes (lawful and otherwise!), they did not have serial numbers removed. Thus, a Magister or a Tiger Moth used for general purposes by a fighter squadron would usually retain its serials whereas a Proctor used for communications duties invariably did not have underwing serials.

An aspect of markings that caused constant bickering between Command, Groups and the Ministry was whether or not the entire cowlings of Oxfords and Ansons should be camouflaged. Throughout the war years one saw evidence of half camouflage and full camouflage irrespective of official orders. There was an obsession about the visibility of yellow training markings, so much so that the spats of Magisters (originally all yellow) were ordered to be camouflaged

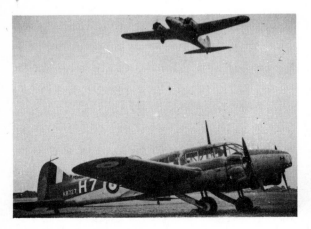

Typical trainer coding is shown on this Anson, K8727, of No 2 FTS. In this 1940 photograph the yellow extends up the aircraft side and the fuselage serial is yellow. 'H' appears on the nose in black.

RAF Camouflage of World War 2

because they were said to shine when seen from above in yellow finish.

Individual aircraft identity markings varied considerably. Although aircraft carried numbers usually within the range one to 150, the addition of letters to distinguish Flights or Squadrons within the Schools — not to mention the precise style of lettering and colouring which varied among units — made some identity of the aircraft holding units possible.

In theory trainer camouflage extended to all trainers in purely non-operational units. Operational Training Units from their inception had aircraft in mixed schemes. Bombers, fighters and many Coastal Command aircraft wore operational colours since OTUs formed a second line force. Ansons, to a late stage of the war, could be seen in OTU hands with either black or yellow under surfaces. Masters — even the two dozen or so armed examples — wore standard trainer camouflage.

An exception came when gliders were introduced for the training of glider pilots. Experimental gliders were ordered to wear the usual training colours applicable to prototypes, etc, except that they were supposed to have eight feet of each wing tip yellow, a rule that was certainly not observed.

When Hotspur and Horsa gliders joined Operational Training Units or Glider Training Schools they had broad black diagonal bands on their yellow under surfaces like target towing aircraft. For a limited time Horsas were flying with underwing serials, white on the black bands and black on the yellow. Some wore a black rectangle to allow display of underwing serials in white. Individual identity was by means of a Sky or pale blue number or letter on the sides of the nose.

Audax, Hector and later Master IIs used as Hotspur tugs had black and yellow striped under surfaces, their upper surfaces, as with training gliders, being Temperate Land Scheme. Whitley tugs at heavy glider training schools retained bomber camouflage, and had Sky or pale blue individual numbers on the sides of the nose until 1943 when standard unit coding was introduced, being Dull Red. By 1944 most Horsas in training units had the standard operational glider finish — Temperate Land Scheme with black under surfaces, sides, fins and rudders. Serials were Dull Red.

Not until 1943 did any appreciable change in trainer markings take place. At the end of 1942 Training Command began to press for changes aimed at making their aircraft, now about in very large numbers, very obvious to other aircraft. One source of worry concerned the number of aircraft undertaking blind approach training — mainly Oxfords with a few Ansons

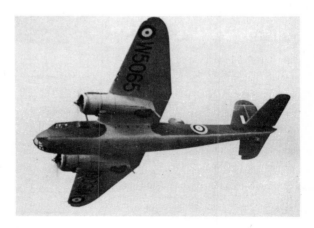

Blackburn Botha W5065 displays the usual underwing serials applied to trainers, during service with No 3 School of General Reconnaissance in mid-1942. Upper surfaces Dark Green and Dark Earth, under surfaces yellow.

Trainers

and Masters. The Blind Approach Training Flights were widely scattered and often based at operational airfields. There seemed a considerable risk of in-flight collisions. In March 1943 it was agreed that some beam approach aircraft should carry large yellow triangles on the nose sides and amidships. No 1 Beam Approach School was first in the field followed by No 1551 Flight and then other BAT Flights. Attempts had been made to get the Ministry to agree to all-yellow or Sky cowlings as identity for these aircraft and those simulating night flying. This was considered to compromise camouflage on the ground. Red was suggested, but the idea died a natural death when the yellow triangles for BAT Flight Oxfords were approved.

A collision in the air at Leuchars on August 8 1943 involving an Anson of No 1510 BAT Flight again highlighted the danger to such aircraft, and the unit requested that BAT Flight machines be yellow overall. The answer was that not all BAT Flights appeared to have applied the very obvious yellow side and nose triangles. In February 1944 these markings were extended by the addition of a yellow triangle on top of the fuselage a few feet aft of the canopy. Even this was deemed insufficient and by June 1944 BAT Flight Oxfords were flying with black triangles outboard of the underwing roundels.

Individual aircraft letters were applied in Sky or white ahead of the fuselage roundels, but some units painted theirs black superimposed upon the yellow nose triangles. These markings were retained until the end of the war, after which the aircraft finally settled for Sky unit code letters.

At Elementary Flying Training Schools there was a steady attrition rate and some collisions, a constant worry to Flying Training Command. In October 1943, with few enemy attacks on airfields and little Luftwaffe activity over Britain, the Command expressed its desire to change markings to the pre-late 1940 style with yellow sides to trainers. The Air Ministry would not

Unit markings on Airspeed Oxford trainers as recorded at the Marshall of Cambridge Civilian Repair Organisation as the aircraft arrived for overhaul, etc. Considerable divergence in style is apparent whilst the camouflage pattern remained very similar although camouflage colours varied. The diagrams depict the following aircraft and units: BL:L4620 recorded February 27 1944 wearing the markings of No 15 (Pilot) Advanced Flying Unit, with which it served from April 21 1942 to February 17 1944; G:DF431 recorded January 30 1944 shortly after leaving No 140 Wing where it had served as a communications aircraft in full trainer markings; LL:DF509 recorded February 12 1944 in the trim of No 2 Air Gunnery School which used the machine from November 7 1942 to February 8 1944; A17:AB654 in the markings of No 12 (P) AFU recorded April 9 1944; DM:AT669 of 15 (P) AFU recorded December 22 1943; R2:V4056 of No 7 Flying Instructors' School recorded April 9 1944. At the head of the right-hand column is the nose of an Oxford of a Blind Approach Training Flight showing the yellow triangles on the side of the nose and above the fuselage, also the late-war yellow wing tips. Sometimes the side triangle carried a black letter or even a motif like a black cat. A black triangle was painted beneath each wing tip, the apex of the solid triangle leading. Such markings were worn, apart from the dorsal triangle, on AT652 'Z' of 1507 BAT Flight on May 31 1943. Below this are: Z:AT652 showing the side marking; EP:T1200 of 20 (P) AFU recorded in May 1944; G:V4043 used by 1518 BAT Flight at Edzell September 22 1942 to September 22 1943 and recorded October 16 1943 (the G in black was outlined white and a similar marking applied to both sides of the nose); WP:AP497 of No 14 (P) AFU recorded April 9 1944; and F4:AP404 of 6 (P) AFU where the machine served from July 1942 to August 1943.

▭ Dark Green	▨ Dark Earth	▦ Dull Blue
▬ Dull Red	░ Yellow	

agree to this, but in December a limited addition of yellow was approved. Yellow would extend up the sides of the cowlings of Tiger Moths and Magisters. From the base of the rear of the cowling to the propeller shaft the lower area would now be yellow. Some EFTSs had already painted a yellow band on the upper surfaces of the wing tips following the wing tip contour. Now the Command was permitted to paint the outer two feet of the upper side of the top wing tip yellow, excluding the ailerons. Yellow bars each one foot wide and extending for three feet were also permitted to be applied flanking the centre of the roundel on the fuselage. Only at EFTSs were these alterations permitted.

It was customary to paint the aircraft identity number Sky, yellow or white on the noses of the elementary trainers. Now these would be black. A few weeks later it became the practice to paint a white outline to the number

Top *Training gliders wore Dark Green/Dark Earth camouflage with yellow and black striped under surfaces. HH464 used by General Aircraft for trials spent most of its time in storage.* **Above** *Ansons were among the aircraft finished in bomber colours but seconded to training like N4995 of 16 OTU in use here in 1940 with black under surfaces.*

where it was applied over the camouflage of the upper surfaces. This did not meet with full Command approval and the next stage was to paint the entire side hinged panels of the cowling on elementary trainers yellow, allowing the identity number to be applied in black. This was approved in March, at which time Command requested that the fuel tank above the mainplane of the Tiger Moths be painted yellow.

Such an additional yellow area was deemed to make the aircraft too con-

RAF Camouflage of World War 2

Master III W8513 has a white serial. It was photographed when in use at the Central Flying School, Little Rissington, where it served from March 1942 to April 1944. '3' is white.

spicuous on the ground and the Air Ministry stated that, if the fuel tanks became yellow, then the yellow wing tips would have to be overpainted. After more wrangling Air Ministry agreed to all the additional yellow areas on Tiger Moths.

In May 1944 it was decided to extend additional yellow trim to Ansons, Harvards, Oxfords and Proctors. Side panels of engine cowlings would now be yellow, but in the case of radial engines only the side areas would be yellow. The outer four feet of the wing tip upper surfaces would be yellow on all trainers including BAT Flight aircraft, and the fuselage would carry a yellow band, the centre line of which passed through the fuselage roundel. Its width was proportional to the roundel, distance being equal to the outer diameter of the blue ring in the roundel.

If any windows prevented the application in this position the band was ordered to be placed midway between the roundel and the tailplane. At the same time the yellow bar marking on the Tiger Moth and Magister, also the yellow Tiger Moth fuel tank, were ordered to be removed. These markings were an alternative to BAT Flight markings in the case of Oxfords, but as might be expected some Oxfords carried the fuselage band in addition to triangles. Flight, or School identity letters and numbers were ordered to be either black or Sky. Flying Training Command did not give up and again requested yellow fuel tanks on Tiger Moths, but this was turned down in June 1944 when the new trim was extended to Ansons and Dominies.

Yellow wing tips and fuselage bands with yellow cowlings were retained until after the end of the war. When, in 1947, trainers adopted a silver finish in preference to the all-yellow trim with black letters which they acquired shortly after the end of the war, the new scheme included yellow bands around the fuselage and wings.

eight

Targets and target-towers

In pre-war days target-towing was undertaken by a variety of aircraft types carrying no particular markings to identify them. Expansion of the RAF brought a special scheme. Aircraft specifically used for target-towing were painted yellow with broad black diagonal striping overall. Serial numbers on wings, fuselage and rudder were white on black, black on yellow areas. These markings were in use when the war broke out, and some were still to be seen in the summer of 1940.

In July 1940 it was decided that the upper surfaces of these aircraft should be camouflaged in Temperate Land Scheme, but that the camouflage should end half way down the fuselage as on training aircraft, leaving the sides black and yellow, three foot black stripes being placed six feet apart. When, in late 1940, the sides of trainers were also camouflaged, this alteration was also made to target towers. Black individual identity letters which had been used were now changed to Medium Grey. During 1941 they were changed to Sky. Similar markings were retained to the end of the war, with the addition of an 18-inch Sky band around the fuselage immediately ahead of the tailplane which was ordered from July 1942. No serials were worn on the under surfaces.

Target-towing was, in 1940, mainly undertaken by Henleys and Battles.

Some of these aircraft were distinguished by a letter-number system such as A-1, A-2 for 'A' Flight and K-1, K-2, etc, for 'K' Flight. During 1941 these tasks were also undertaken by Lysanders wearing the late 1940 scheme. They were joined first by the Defiant target tug and in mid-summer 1942 by the Miles Martinet, both of which flew in the Temperate Land Scheme with black and yellow under surfaces and Sky band and codes.

In March 1942 a Sky rear fuselage band was applied to Hampdens and Wellingtons of the bomber Group target-towing flights to readily distinguish them as target-towers, although they did not wear black and yellow stripes. In October 1944 the Vengeance TT IV was introduced in the standard target towing colour scheme.

Sundry other aircraft used for target-towing and general towing work also had black/yellow bands on their under surfaces. Miles Aircraft produced towed targets for use at the end of the war, and these were black with yellow trim. In October 1944 the upper surface of the wing tips of Martinets were painted yellow, which extended four feet in from the tip, but not many wore this feature and it does not seem to have been applied to other target towers.

Throughout the war, DH Queen Bee aircraft were used for anti-aircraft gunnery, particularly from Towyn in South Wales. Before the war radio-controlled Queen Bees were silver with black serials and when the war began their upper surfaces became Temperate Land in colour. Serials were usually absent from under surfaces and were again when in August 1940 the under surfaces of pilotless aircraft became Sky, a colour worn to the end of the war. Some had Type A and later C underwing roundels, but there was no hard rule about this and generally roundels were absent.

nine

Aircraft overseas

Middle East

Until late 1940 camouflage colouring on aircraft in the Middle East was similar to that of home-based aircraft, although there was some experimentation with tan shades by units in the area. Nevertheless, upper surfaces of Dark Green and Dark Earth with black lower surfaces were standard on bombers in 1940, in the summer of which day bombers acquired Sky under surfaces.

Night bombers and Bombay bomber-transports retained black under surfaces including those of the latter type of aircraft when used for night bombing. Roundel positions and types were similar to those on home-based aircraft, although quite a lot of

Liberator B VI BZ990:Z̲ of No 355 Squadron photographed at Salbani in May 1944. Finish is the original American Olive Drab/Neutral Grey. 'Z̲', 'SNAKE' and 'BZ990' appear in black (W. Munday).

Artwork on the nose of a night bomber Liberator VI in the Middle East in 1945 (Stuart Middleton).

machines in the Middle East had Type A1 roundels on their upper surfaces well into the war whereas machines being delivered from Britain seem to have retained roundels worn previously.

Supply problems with Sky dope led to a variety of tones of blue but, as Blenheim IVs began to reach the Command from Britain, together with supplies of Hurricanes in the latest mid-1940 finish, then the aircraft in the Middle East and Malta came into line with those at home. For longer than at home, fighters in the desert retained half black under surfaces with white and later with shades of blue. During the summer of 1940 Sky under surfaces gradually came into vogue.

The same colours were to be seen in East Africa where Wellesleys used for day operations had Sky under surfaces. One squadron mixed two shades of tan for application to the

upper surfaces of Wellesleys and Gordons on its charge.

The green and brown finish was quite unsuitable for desert areas where most of the fighting was taking place. As early as August 1940 Blenheims were being ferried to the Middle East with the Dark Green of their upper surfaces replaced by a tan shade, but it was August 1941 before a new colour scheme for the theatre was finally promulgated. Green areas in upper camouflage would now be changed to Middle Stone and under surfaces Azure Blue, these colours applying to fighters, day bombers and some transports.

Since they needed maximum camouflage when on the ground, night bombers also acquired Dark Earth/Mid Stone finish with black

under surfaces which were steadily extended up the sides of bombers in late 1940.

Maritime strike aircraft in part adopted these colours but their under surfaces were usually black for night operations and sometimes Azure Blue if they operated mainly by day. By 1942 maritime aircraft usually wore the same colours as home-based machines, although again some are known to have had the two brown colours on the upper surfaces. Some Beaufighters in use in 1943 had Azure Blue under surfaces with two-tone brown upper surfaces when used on

Blenheim 1 L4827 coded MU and of 60 Squadron in the Far East, during operations in the defence of Malaya in 1941.

A Spitfire of No 145 Squadron in the Middle East (G. R. S. McKay).

strike operations.

Squadron letters were usually white on fighters, although red and blue were also employed and some individualistic markings appeared (more than would ever have been permitted at home). Not all squadrons carried unit codes, some merely applying individual letters to their aircraft. Serials were generally black, but in 1942 in keeping with home-based aircraft, bombers in the Middle East acquired red serials and codes in favour of Medium Grey.

The colouring of aircraft in the Middle East was affected by the arrival of

Blenheim VDs, possibly of No 114 Squadron in north-west Africa, wearing Middle East colours. 'L' appears in white. The serial is BA4 . . .

American types of aircraft. Although many were painted in Dark Earth/Middle Stone/Azure Blue, later arrivals including Liberators and some Marauders remained in the standard American colours, for the war was by then moving away from the desert.

Up to their withdrawal from operations Wellington 1cs, IIIs and Xs had Dark Earth/Middle Stone/black finish, even though by then they were flying from Italian bases.

In North West Africa the colouring of fighters was as in the desert, but when the fighter squadrons advanced into Italy their aircraft generally switched to Ocean Grey/Dark Green/Medium Sea Grey with white or Sky codes. Night fighters wore either the same colouring as those in Britain in 1943 or were Medium Sea Grey/Dark Green

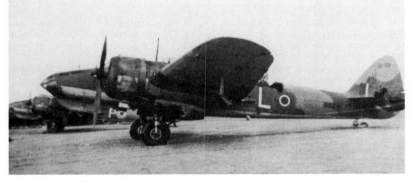

Spitfire IX NH346 with white coding LK:M in the Middle East in 1945. Previously it served with Nos 412 and 485 Squadrons (G. R. S. McKay).

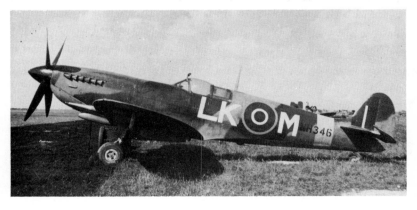

Beaufighter LX876 of No 27 Squadron wears Far East roundels and rudder stripe, and has a SNAKE prefix to its serial.

with black under surfaces, whereas in 1942 they had worn two-tone brown upper surfaces with Azure or black under surfaces. Code letters were generally red and often serials too.

Dakota transports used in increasing numbers in the Middle East from 1943 had Olive Drab/Neutral Grey finish, but some wore tan/Neutral Grey worn by many American C-47s. RAF Dakotas usually had red codes and black serials.

Trainers in the Middle East wore the same finish as those at home until their upper surfaces were changed to Dark Earth/Middle Stone. Unit identity markings were Sky, red or yellow. Communications aircraft wore either yellow or Azure Blue under surfaces.

Far East

As in the Middle East, aircraft in the Far East at the start of the war had similar colouring to home-based aircraft. There were no fighters in India or Malaya, but a number of Blenheim 1 bombers in Dark Green/Dark Earth/black finish. They did not lose their underwing serials in 1939 and it was some months before the Type A1 roundels were changed, but in 1940 roundels came into line with home-based aircraft styles. Grey code letters had been worn since the start of the war.

At the time of the Japanese attack in Malaya, Blenheims were still mainly wearing black under surfaces, but reinforcement aircraft from the Middle East wore Sky or Azure Blue, this also being true of Hurricanes. Buffaloes in use by this time wore Dark Green/Dark Earth/Sky finish with grey codes. They had Sky rear fuselage bands and spinners.

Following the fall of Singapore and the Dutch islands, the main aircraft types in India were Hurricanes and Blenheim Mk IVs, both types settling for Dark Green/Dark Earth/Sky finish with grey unit markings, although some aircraft from the Middle East are known to have retained the colours of that theatre. Vengeance dive bombers in Dark Green/Dark Earth/Sky (or Azure) replaced the Blenheims.

Next came Hurricane fighter-bombers and Spitfire VIIIs in Dark Green/Dark Earth with Medium Sea Grey under surfaces, white identity letters and often white serials. In support of them were Republic P-47 Thunderbolts. Early deliveries were Olive Drab/Neutral Grey, but when these were taken in for overhauls they often emerged in British paints mixed in comparable colours. By the end of the war many of the Thunderbolts had shed their camouflage for natural finish with Olive Drab anti-dazzle panels.

In 1943 large code letters were replaced by smaller sized ones on the fighters, often only 18 inches high. As a further aid to identity white spinners, white bands encircling the mainplanes and a white stripe across the fin above the tail stripe were painted on camou-

RAF Camouflage of World War 2

Top *Blenheim VD BA612 in the finish approved for coastal reconnaissance aircraft to be used in the Middle East – Extra Dark Sea Grey/white. The machine served in the Middle East between November 1943 and August 1944.* Right *Lysander L4677 in Middle East camouflage of Dark Earth/Mid Stone/Azure Blue.*

flaged fighters. These latter markings came into use early 1944 and on 'silver' Thunderbolts they were ordered to be dark blue but often were black. Wing bands on the Thunderbolts were ordered to be 28 inches wide. 18-inch bands were painted around the tailplane and across the fin the band was 17 inches wide. A black or blue leading edge was applied to the cowling. White or black/blue bands on the wings did not overlap the flaps.

As in the Middle East and Indian Ocean areas, aircraft used for coastal and oversea patrol wore the Temper-ate Sea Scheme/white finish which later became Extra Dark Sea Grey/white which in the Middle East applied to flying-boats, Wellingtons, Venturas and Baltimores. In the Far East it also applied to Catalinas, but to some of those of No 209 Squadron a special scheme was applied — black on the upper surfaces, for the aircraft performed some clandestine operations. Another interesting exception concerned the Mosquito IVs of No 618 Squadron ear-marked for Highball operations in the Pacific area. Their finish was Dark Green/Ocean Grey with Azure Blue under surfaces.

ten

Roundels and fin stripes

British roundels used during the war fell into three forms. The basic roundel was Type A with a red central disc, in diameter the equal of the width of the white band around which an outer surround in blue was painted. Type A1 roundel was the Type A with a yellow outer ring and proportions as before, although in 1940 some aircraft had a narrow outer yellow ring because the depth of the fuselage did not allow a wide one around the existing Type A. Almost all wartime RAF aircraft had above each wing tip a Type B roundel, blue with a red centre which was two-fifths of the diameter of the outer ring. This was sometimes known as the night flying roundel, a title dating from use earlier exclusively on night bombers.

In July 1942 a new roundel was introduced, Type C, in which the blue and red areas were enlarged leaving a very narrow white ring which, in the case of the Type C1 roundel, was also true of the yellow outer ring. Such roundels were in use until three years after the war.

In September 1939 the standard roundel in use on British-based aircraft on the fuselage and above the wing tips was Type B. It came into general use about March 1939, but many training aircraft retained Type A on their fuselage sides and wing under surfaces.

There was soon dissatisfaction with Type B roundels once the war had started. A white ring was therefore added, converting them to Type A on the fuselage sides. Bombers were already wearing these beneath their wing tips and some fighters had them, although this never seems to have been authorised. The official instruction for the change to Type A came on November 10 1939, but such roundels were in use well before this date. All fighters in France were flying with Type A fuselage and underwing roundels by November 1939, and bombers there had them until their withdrawal from France.

On November 6 1939 all operational general reconnaissance landplanes in Coastal Command were ordered to add a white ring to upper surface roundels. This was soon extended to flying-boats and training aircraft in the Command. Type A roundels above the wings, whilst making the aircraft easier to see when over water, clearly revealed them on their airfields.

In mid-February 1940 trials were begun at Thorney Island with a narrower white band in the wing roundels and a vertical yellow stripe on the rudder of an Anson. March saw trials on Anson PK:G wearing Type A fuselage roundels outlined as pre-war in yellow and a yellow stripe on its rudder. This bright roundel rendered the stripe unnecessary. Rudder colours were in any case rejected because extra dope on a control surface upset its delicate balance. For a similar reason wing roundels never overlapped the ailerons although they were applied as large as possible and inset on the upper surfaces about one-sixth of the wing span — ie one third on each wing. Under the wings roundels were usually closer to the wing tip than those above.

Consideration was also now given to the painting of a stripe or roundels on the fixed portion of the tailplane. A bright yellow fin was considered during April 1940. Further tests were made on an Anson which had yellow outlines to Type A fuselage roundels, a yellow band around the rear fuselage and a yellow fin stripe.

As a result of these and other trials it was resolved that Type A1 roundels should be carried on the fuselages of all home-based aircraft, and that the fin should carry red/white/blue stripes, red foremost. These did not always cover the entire fin, but on fighters and smaller bombers this was often the case. Some units opted for narrower stripes. The stripes did not cover the rudder or its hinges.

On smaller aircraft Type A1 roundels sometimes had a very narrow yellow band. This also applied to some night bombers which had these and very small fin stripes to reduce them from being seen at night. A smaller band also reduced man hours needed in applying the new roundels. On trainers, which had yellow sides, only the top segment of the roundel needed to be applied by a band equal in width to the other bands in the roundel.

Fighters were all ordered to wear Type A roundels and in May 1940 it was ordered that the roundel under the black half of the wing must be outlined yellow and be as large as possible. The yellow ring was to be not less than one quarter of the width of the blue ring.

From May 1 1940 all RAF aircraft were ordered to carry fin stripes, although this feature had been introduced some weeks previously. In France fighters of the Air Component had worn rudder stripes, blue foremost — despite their effect upon balance — to help the French identify them. These were now ordered to be standard, and on the fin, with red leading.

When, on June 7 1940, Sky under surfaces were ordered for all fighters, the instruction was that roundels on this surface would all be removed. Confusion arose at a time when fighting was intense and shortage of Sky dope meant that many fighters continued to have black/white under surfaces and roundels. Despite the order fighters were flying throughout the summer of 1940 with underwing roundels.

An order was issued on July 19 1940 that all GR aircraft would now have Type B upper wing roundels, red and blue rings being extended over white areas. Then, on July 20, it was ordered that *all* aircraft would carry Type A underwing roundels

except for fighters, and Whitleys operated exclusively at night. Wellingtons and Hampdens set aside for day operations would have Type A underwing roundels, the white rings of which could be overpainted for night operations. What credence can be placed upon these official orders is highly questionable for some bombers had kept Type A underwing roundels since before the war. Blenheims usually had them.

During July 1940 quite a lot of night bombers had the white of their fuselage Type A1 roundels and fin stripes overpainted grey or with a black wash. Yellow rings were similarly doctored in 1940 and 1941.

Aircraft used for searchlight co-operation duties had Type A1 roundels on their black under surfaces. Spitfires of the PDU had Type A roundels above and below the wings, whilst on the fuselage they carried Type A1 roundels at this time. There was a period when such aircraft had Type B roundels and fin stripes red/blue. Later in the war they settled for Type B upper wing roundels and red/-white/blue fuselage roundels and fin flashes.

By July 1940 a considerable assortment of roundels by colour and size existed, and the modeller needs to watch very carefully whether the machine he models actually had the prescribed roundels.

On July 4 a conference was held to discuss markings generally. It decided that all fuselage roundels would now be Type A1 with bands of equal width. Overall sizes at the time varied much. Since enemy aircraft had crosses beneath their wings it was decided that RAF aircraft, apart from trainers and communications aircraft, would carry none to aid quick recognition. 'RAF roundels' were, it was admitted, likely to be a tonic for the population when they saw them, but operational needs had to come first. However, many fighters had them and to start major repainting at the height of battle did not make sense so it was soon decided to retain them.

Many Coastal Command aircraft

now operated at night as well as by day. Many had black under surfaces and these carried no roundels. Blenheim fighters which operated by day, however, did have underwing Type A roundels.

Thus, the Battle of Britain was fought by fighters wearing Type A1 fuselage roundels, Type B above the wings and Type A underwing roundels in profusion of sizes — usually as large as possible. Night bombers had Type A1 fuselage roundels in which white and yellow rings were often over-painted with a grey or black wash. They had Type B upper wing roundels and some had Type A under their wing tips. As with so many facets of markings, observations one made at the time do not always accord with official documents.

Fin stripes varied considerably in the summer of 1940. In July of that year it was agreed that these should conform to a size of 27 inches high with three bands each eight inches wide, and this seems largely to have been adhered to, certainly after the Battle.

When, in November 1940, the port under surfaces of the wings of fighters were changed to black, the roundel thereon was outlined yellow, bands varying in width. This feature was retained until black surfaces reverted to Sky.

Briefly, after night fighters were

Typical code letter and serial presentation is shown on Lancaster QR:N-5724 of No 61 Squadron photographed after a belly landing at Wittering on September 28 1942. Despite illustrations that have purported to show the style used for the application of letters and numerals, these often differed in shape from those authorised. R5724 joined No 106 Squadron on July 6 1972 and passed to No 61 Squadron immediately. It was damaged in battle on September 25 1942.

painted all black in 1940-41, they wore Type A roundels under their wing tips. Again the squadrons involved doctored some of their fuselage roundels and fin stripes, applying black washes over bright areas to the start of 1942.

March 1941 saw the arrival of the Fortress 1 high-altitude bombers for No 2 Group. These posed problems markings-wise. They carried Type B upper wing roundels. Type A1 on the fuselage but no underwing roundels. By this period it was unusual to see roundels under the wings of day bombers.

Another type which brought exceptions to marking schemes was the Whitley. Instructions had been adhered to since the start of the war that these aircraft should not carry underwing roundels. When No 4 Group pressed ahead and painted a high proportion of its Whitleys all black, the question of suitable roundels arose. The Air Ministry ordained that they should have standard roundel types, but like other Groups 4 Group gave permission for the white and yellow areas in national markings to be modified. Soon some Whitley squadrons had aircraft bearing only Type B roundels and the white in fin flashes painted out.

In the early months of the war roundel colours had been bright and the finish quite glossy to make them easily visible. In the summer of 1940 bombers began to wear subdued colours and two duller shades, Dull Blue which was a greyish blue and Dull Red which had a rusty brown appearance. My first notes on the observance of these new colours were made in July 1940 when I saw some Wellingtons wearing the new tones. These were obviously exceptional at the time and months later the old bright colours were still in vogue. These dull colours were retained until after the war.

The whole question of suitable roundels for the mid-war period was raised in October 1941. What was needed were roundels distinctive yet not over conspicuous, and certainly not so conspicuous that they were visible before ready identification of the aircraft type was possible. Ideally they should become visible at the same time as an aircraft outline. In the case of Type A1 the roundel was visible when the aircraft was far away.

In the closing weeks of 1941 trials were undertaken, mainly at Farnborough, to devise a new roundel to accord with these foregoing ideas. It was decided that by widening the proportions of the red and blue areas, and reducing the white and yellow to narrow bands, the desired effect could be achieved. In practice this meant that, for instance, if the centre Dull Red disc had a diameter of 12 inches it would be surrounded by a two-inch white band, an eight-inch blue band and this outlined by a two-inch yellow band making a roundel with an overall diameter of 36 inches. Such roundels were known as Type C and Type C1 when

the outer yellow surround was included.

Fin flashes too were modified so that the white stripe was always two inches wide whilst adjacent stripes on fighters of blue and red were each 11 inches wide and 24 inches high. Larger aircraft had these two colours 17 inches wide whilst on small aircraft they were eight inches wide. Three sizes of Type C/C1 roundels were prescribed. These new roundels were ordered to be introduced on July 1 1942.

By 1942 there was more systematic application of all markings than hitherto. Night bombers had Type B wing roundels on upper surfaces, Type A1/C1 on their fuselages and 27 inch high/24 inch wide fin stripes. By the end of winter, doctored toned-down roundels had become a rare sight.

Day bombers wore the same style roundels and flashes as night bombers without underwing roundels, although the inevitable exception spoilt the rule as, for example, a Mosquito IV seen with Type C underwing roundels. Fighters had Type B upper wing roundels, Type C1 fuselage roundels and Type C under surface roundels. On night fighters there were never any underwing roundels. Trainers and communication aircraft wore the same roundel arrangements as fighters. Coastal Command aircraft in 1942 settled for fuselage and wing roundels. Roundel types and positions were standardised in the Middle East to accord with those on home-based aircraft.

From July 1942 to the end of hostilities roundels on home-based aircraft were unchanged in style and little in general positioning as the following summary shows:

Fighters Type B above wings, C1 on fuselage, C below wings (absent on night fighters). From January 3 1945 many fighters in 2TAF, fighter-bombers, PR aircraft and light bombers had Type C upper wing roundels and later still Type C1. Mosquitoes and 2 Group bombers did not wear underwing roundels.

Bombers Type B above wings, C1 on fuselage sides. A few bombers had Type C wing roundels before the war ended.

Coastal Command aircraft Type B wing roundels, C1 on fuselage.

Transports, trainers, communications aircraft, target towers Type B wing roundels, Type C under wing tips, Type C1 on fuselage. Transport Albemarles did not carry underwing roundels. Transports in bomber colours did not have underwing roundels, nor operational gliders.

Pilotless aircraft Type B above wings, Type C1 on fuselage. Some had Type C underwing roundels.

Anti-aircraft co-operation aircraft Type B above wings, Type C1 on fuselage and on wing under surfaces (when the latter were black as was the case with some Oxfords which occasionally were finished black overall).

Roundels in the Far East

In April 1943 AHQ India expressed its concern about national identity markings. Mainly due to dope fading, the blue ring in roundels merged with the camouflage on upper surfaces leaving only the red disc. This had led to incidents between British aircraft, with Mohawks being mistaken for Mitsubishi Zeros. A yellow outline for Type B roundels was suggested, but this would have revealed aircraft on the ground and not be in keeping with roundel styles. Type A roundels were then suggested.

Meanwhile the Royal Australian Air Force, having encountered similar troubles, had adopted a white disc surrounded by blue as its national marking. In May 1943 AHQ India expressed a wish to adopt this style. With further incidents AHQ India took the initiative in mid-June and adopted the Australian style which became standard from June 26 when London gave its approval.

White was very conspicuous in the roundels, which were often applied quite small. Standard sizes were agreed: (i) small — white six inches diameter, blue 16 inches; (ii) medium — white nine inches in diameter and blue 32 inches; (iii) large — white nine inches diameter and blue 48 inches. No change was made in the height of fin stripes in which white led, but the white would now be either: (i) 16 inches wide with a six-inch blue stripe; (ii) nine inches wide with a 15-inch blue stripe; or (iii) nine inches wide with a 27-inch wide blue stripe. Since it seemed unlikely that aircraft in the Middle East, Persian Gulf or Aden would ever meet Japanese aircraft they retained standard roundels and fin flashes.

eleven

Special markings and exceptions

What makes a study of markings always so interesting is that although the schemes were usually applied as laid down, exceptions are extensive. Modifications were always common, colours so often different, that it is true to say that no two aircraft looked really alike as regards their finish. Different dope sources, different dope manufacturers, different mixing — not to mention weathering, all these played a part, as ever. Very precise measurements were planned by manufacturers for camouflage patterns but few were slavishly followed.

Photographs are an essential source for modelling. The most interesting photographs are often to be found among those privately taken during the war and often resting in a long lost photo album. It is well worth asking around the family and among friends to see just what does exist. Quite often rare and unique material turns up. Who knows, you may find a shot of a Wellington VI in squadron hands or a Welkin of AFDU!

Inevitably in any search one seems sooner or later to come across some item quite overlooked or unrecorded in the welter of booklets on markings now available. I well remember a squadron of Spitfires racing low overhead in the summer of 1943. It seemed impossible, but their upper surfaces were all Dark Green, undersides a dark shade of grey. Their Dull Red squadron codes were LN. Which squadron, what was the purpose? Somewhere, someone must know the answer. These were quite typical of many exceptions to the rule that one saw, yet now one feels bound to question the truth of what one *knows* one saw.

A class of aircraft that always wore a variety of markings were those which were 'experimental'. Prior to 1941 they wore a wide assortment of finishes. A typical oddity was the prototype Mosquito W4050 which first flew in an overall all-yellow scheme with Type A roundels. Early in 1941 its upper surfaces became Dark Green and Dark Earth in keeping with an official edict

Typical of a prototype, the Welkin DG556 has Ocean Grey/Dark Green finish with yellow undersurfaces and 'P' marking in yellow. The long range tanks are a hitherto unpublished feature.

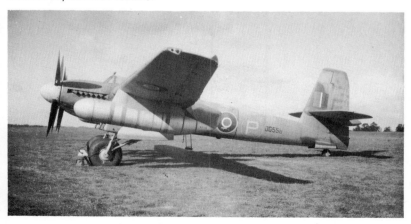

Airspeed Horsa gliders. PF800 wore the full array of AEAF stripes on its standard bomber camouflage colours. Dark shading in the upper surface camouflage represent Dark Green, the paler Dark Earth. Serials were red. PF800 was delivered to 38 MU on March 20 1944 and was lost in action during the Normandy night landing June 5/6 1944. PW878, which did not wear any 'invasion markings', was delivered May 1 1944 and flying in the hands of the ORTU took part in Operation Varsity, the Rhine crossing assault, March 24 1945 (Drawings by George Burn).

RAF Camouflage of World War 2

Mosquito NF XIII, possibly MM504, photographed at Le Culot October 5 1944. Despite official instructions the AEAF stripes have partly obliterated the serial and unit letters of this 409 squadron machine. The AEAF stripes are also incomplete (R. H. Finlayson).

on prototype markings of January 1941. A further instruction of January 1 1941 was that prototype aircraft would carry a yellow 'P' marking outlined by a thin yellow circle whose diameter equalled that of the outside diameter of the fuselage roundel.

Later in 1941 it became the practice to paint the upper surfaces of prototypes in the colouring the type would wear when in its operational role, so that prototype Spitfires from August 1941 would have Dark Green and grey upper surfaces and the prototype Hornet Medium Grey upper surfaces, whilst yellow under surfaces were to be worn by all prototypes.

Flying-boats, apart from the half-scale Saro Shrimp which flew in a finish of Extra Dark Sea Grey and Dark Green with yellow under surfaces and merely carried a letter P, wore standard operational colours because painting then in a special scheme was such a considerable task. Usually they had the 'P in a circle' marking.

Some captured enemy aircraft like the Messerschmitt Bf 110 AX772 and Heinkel He 111 AW177 acquired Dark Green and Dark Earth upper surfaces

and yellow under surfaces but no prototype marking. Others retained Luftwaffe camouflage on their upper surfaces whilst having yellow under surfaces. Messerschmitt Me 410 TF209 captured in Italy was shipped to Britain and repainted Dark Green/Dark Earth/yellow and carried the full 'P in a circle' marking. On the other hand the Heinkel He 177 TS439 captured in France was flown to Farnborough wearing French roundels which were changed then to British roundels. This large machine, which kept its full German finish, had a 'P in a circle' marking and full AEAF stripes.

Special tactical markings existed both for operations and exercises. They appear to have been first used during the war on army co-operation aircraft in 1941 when, for a short period, some wore half black undersides. Similar markings were carried on sundry other exercises and notably during the large scale Exercise *Spartan* in March 1943. Half the force employed had part of their under surfaces painted with black distemper and a one-foot wide stripe along the forward fuselage. A variation of this scheme came into use for Operation *Starkey* in September 1943. Black and white bands were painted around the wings of some aircraft used. Variations again were seen, whereby some aircraft had the bands mid-placed between the wings and fuselage. Others had narrow bands around their wing tips.

Special markings and exceptions

From June 5 1944 all aircraft tactically employed in connection with the D-Day landings were ordered to have black and white stripes painted around their wings and rear fuselages. Single-engined aircraft had five 18-inch wide black and white bands (two black, three white) ordered to end six inches inboard of the underwing roundels and 18 inches ahead of any fuselage Sky band.

Twin-engined aircraft had bands 24 inches wide around the wings and 20 inches wide around the fuselage. The markings were supposed not to blot out unit coding, but there were cases where this happened.

Stripes were carried by fighters, fighter-bombers, tactical bombers, strike fighters, some PR aircraft and transports including gliders.

Seen from above, aircraft wearing the stripes were highly conspicuous when on the ground. Therefore by autumn many aircraft merely wore them on the under sides of the rear fuselage, although even at the end of

the war one saw machines with the full array.

Black and white stripes were not a new feature. Since they so resembled Focke-Wulf Fw 190s from certain angles, and were pitted against the German aircraft when these were attacking targets on the British coast, Typhoons wore tactical markings. In November 1942 they were ordered to have four black and three white bands under each wing painted on from the wing root. Each black stripe was a foot wide and the intervening white stripes each two feet wide. For a time Typhoons wore a yellow band across the upper surface of each mainplane. In a few cases two such bands were painted across each mainplane. A few Typhoons had white noses ahead of the wing, and a variation existed in No 181 Squadron whereby the radiator casing was Sky.

Tempest Vs which entered service in the early spring of 1944 also wore the black and white stripes but all were removed during April 1944 since they

Typifying an aircraft of the Allies in RAF service, Boston IV OA:B-BZ443 has a red nose 'B' trimmed yellow, the Cross of Lorraine French motif and red/white/blue French rudder striping. The crewman in the foreground wears a dark blue uniform and French cap as he attends to the 500 pounders. BZ443 was with 342 Squadron from September to November 1944 when it went to No 88 Squadron before returning after a few days to 342 Squadron who kept it until March 1945.

RAF Camouflage of World War 2

Some Liberator IIIs supplied to the RAF retained Olive Drab/Neutral Grey US colours, like LV337 seen here. This machine was used for service trials in the spring of 1942. Note that the type of film used has made the red centres to the roundels, and the red stripe on the fin flashes, appear white.

were similar to the AEAF stripes proposed for use on D-Day.

Since the end of 1943 P-51s of the USAAF had been flying with white noses, wing bands and tail stripes as a special identity feature. In February 1944 similar markings were extended to the RAF's Mustang IIIs used now to aid in the escort of American B-17s and B-24s on deep penetrations of Germany. RAF Mustangs had a foot wide white band across the fin and rudder 18 inches from the fin tip, 15-inch wide tailplane bands 30 inches from the tip, a 15-inch band around each mainplane set about 15 feet from the wing tips, and a 12-inch band around the nose immediately aft of the propeller. These markings were retained to about D-Day after which the tail stripes were deleted. Spinners were usually white.

Mosquito *Oboe* leaders acquired two thin white bands which encircled the fuselage adjacent to the roundels. A few Mosquito pathfinders had full AEAF stripes since they operated in a tactical role after D-Day. Lancasters used in 1945 as *GEE-H* bombing leaders had two yellow stripes painted on the outer faces of each fin of Lancas-

ters of 3 Group in 1945. Yellow was also used as an outline for code letters on aircraft of No 5 Group which, by the end of the war, had also painted its code and individual letters above the tailplanes of some of its Lancasters, some of which had the letters repeated under the tailplane.

In November 1943 trials were held to use camouflage as a means of destroying the outline of aircraft. A Mosquito was painted to look like a Typhoon or Spitfire, but the idea never progressed far, like the use of browns and greys for fighter camouflage.

An unusual fighter scheme was worn by some Meteors on the Continent which were painted white overall for tactical reasons. Other schemes for Meteors in 1944-45 were the standard fighter colour and Ocean Grey/Dark Green with yellow undersurfaces. Like other fighters thus employed, Meteors used against V-1 flying bombs usually did not have yellow wing leading edges.

Aircraft flying with crews of Occupied countries usually wore a small emblem showing them to be Dutch, Czech, Polish, Norwegian or French, based upon national aircraft markings or a national symbol.

The addition of 'personal' markings was always frowned upon by the authorities, nevertheless some aircraft did have them although it is wrong to imagine that more than a small percentage wore such trimmings.

Between 1940 and 1942 some aircraft, particularly in second line formations, had an 18-inch square painted on the top of the rear fuselage. This was a gas detection marking, pale green or brown, which would show black spots when gas was present. Gas laying was part of the role assigned to No 2 Group, but they never used it. They did operate producing smoke screens and for this purpose on D-Day Bostons of the Group had their noses painted white to make them obvious to naval gunners.

Whereas the Americans flew many aircraft in natural metal finish, by the end of the war few RAF aircraft had this. One exception apart from Mustangs was a Spitfire seen at Cranfield in 1944. Such exceptions to the rule were to be seen throughout the war, like one Magister painted yellow overall carrying large areas of Dark Earth camouflage, in use in 1942 and curiously coded ZN:IP.

An interest in markings is as fascinating as any, the scope of the hobby vast. A model collection portraying the history of camouflage suggests itself, or a series of models of one type showing the variations in markings would make an excellent thematic collection. Why should stamp collectors have it all their own way?